By Susan Elnicki Wade and Bill Wade

www.weloveoysters.com

This book is dedicated to

Max & Nicholas,
for being our greatest love and inspiration

© Copyright 2015
All rights reserved. No part of this book may be reproduced, transmitted, or stored in an information retrieval system in any form or by any means, graphic, electronic, or mechanical, including photocopying, taping, & recording, without prior written permission from the publisher.

ISBN: 978-1-5194-9520-4

Authors: Susan Elnicki Wade and Bill Wade
Photographs: Susan Elnicki Wade
Maps: Bill Wade
Cover Design: Joe Barsin at Citizen Pride
Web Site Design: Zach Howard at Exton Edge

Printed in the United States of America

Also by Susan and Bill Wade:
Crab Decks & Tiki Bars of the Chesapeake Bay
Maryland and Virginia Editions

Chesapeake Oyster Lovers' Handbook
2916 Northampton Street, NW
Washington, DC 20015
(202) 531-7135
susan@crabdecksandtikibars.com
bill@crabdecksandtikibars.com

www.weloveoysters.com

Table of Contents

Introduction v

Pearls of Wisdom
New Oyster Cult: Celebrate the Bay's Epic Comeback Tour 3
Oysters Sidekicks: Cocktails Required, Toppings Optional 8
Discover the Harmony of Oysters & Bay Culture 11
Baltimore & Its Oyster: A Trip Down Memory Lane.................13

Chesapeake Oyster Houses & Raw Bars

MARYLAND
Baltimore 17
Northern Maryland 59
Annapolis 79
DC's Maryland Suburbs & Southern Maryland.............97
The Eastern Shore 123

WASHINGTON, DC...149

VIRGINIA
Northern Virginia 201
Virginia Peninsulas..237
Virginia Beach & Norfolk 255

Chesapeake Aquafarms & Oyster Brands 281

Index to Oyster Houses, Brands & Aquafarms 321

Chesapeake Oyster Taste Chart............................. 327

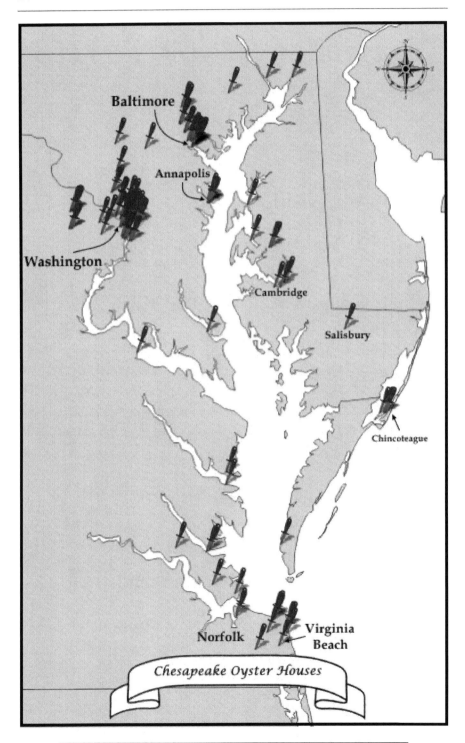

Introduction

The concept for this book began a few years ago during a moms' getaway trip to New York City. My best gal Brenda and I were lounging at the Grand Central Oyster Bar, marveling at the elegant tiles and arched vaulted ceiling.

The oyster list was long and impressive. Plenty of options were on hand for bivalves from the East and West coasts, but only one came from the Chesapeake Bay. When I asked the barkeep why my home region was so poorly represented, he shrugged his shoulders and said that nobody asked for them. Two businessmen, who were killing time until a commuter train delivered them to their suburban nests, decided to chime in on the conversation. "Order our local oysters," they insisted. "They're the best in the world."

Our unexpected bar companions had never tasted a Chesapeake oyster, believing that they were too salty, nearly extinct and grown in polluted waters. Having heard this misconception before, I decided to put Bay oysters to the test and see how they measured up against "the best." I asked the shucker to set up an oyster challenge with Rappahannocks from Virginia, Blue Points from Connecticut and Kumamotos from the Pacific Northwest — but not tell us which was which. A blind tasting of each region's envoy would determine the winner.

We worked clockwise around the icy tray, slurping and savoring the delicate flavors of each oyster. Brenda, who is allergic to oysters but always a good sport, acted as referee and kept track of the ratings. The decision was unanimous. When all three tasters indicated a favorite, the shucker proclaimed the Chesapeake oyster was victorious.

As the newly converted Bay bivalve enthusiasts rushed off to catch their train, I felt proud of my regional oysters' performance, but I left with a nagging sense of dismay that Chesapeake oysters are misunderstood and underrated.

When I returned home and told my husband Bill about the oyster challenge results, he reacted with true Maryland pride and could not imagine any other outcome. He fondly remembered wintry days at his father's house in Lusby, MD, when wild oysters were plentiful and a central part of family gatherings. His dad would bring home dozens of oysters, often carried in an old cardboard box, and the men convened in the garage to shuck. They'd drink a few brews and shoot the breeze while opening shells for the evening meal.

Eating oysters was more than a cherished regional ritual. They encompassed the unique Chesapeake lifestyle and offered a tangible symbol for the resolute spirit of the Bay. Sure, they'd fallen upon hard times, and the oyster population had dropped, but it was difficult for us to believe that the days of relishing Bay oysters were now distant memories.

And so began our journey to rediscover the local oyster. We talked to watermen and restaurant owners we'd met during our travels for the Crab Decks & Tiki Bars books. We scoured the Bay for oyster houses and found bivalves being shucked in the most unlikely places. High-end swanky restaurants in downtown DC, suburban strip malls, fish markets in Baltimore, dock bars on the Maryland waterfront, glittery nightclubs and even a general store in Virginia were filled with people eagerly serving and devouring Bay oysters.

When expanding our research to the sources who are harvesting oysters, we encountered a brilliant new breed of watermen who are crafting innovative methods for growing bivalves in aquafarms along the shores. Their enthusiasm for creating sustainable and abundant oysters was contagious.

Most of all we found hope that the Chesapeake oyster is not a relic of the past. In fact, it's back with gusto. A resurrection is taking place with oyster houses popping up all around the region, and upscale Manhattan bars now bragging about their Chesapeake oysters on the half shell. The word is spreading, and people are swooning over Bay bivalves.

Chesapeake Oyster Lovers' Handbook is our gift of thanks to the people who fought to save this local seafood delicacy and our present to everyone who is ready to undertake a Chesapeake oyster adventure.

— Susan and Bill Wade

About this Book

After publishing four editions of *Crab Decks & Tiki Bars of the Chesapeake Bay*, we are pleased to announce our latest endeavor, *Chesapeake Oyster Lovers' Handbook*. This new book is the indispensable guide to everything oyster on the Bay, covering oyster houses, raw bars, aquafarms and bivalve brands in Maryland, Virginia and Washington, DC.

It's your passport to buck-a-shuck happy hours, oyster pub crawls and kitchens that tuck crispy fried oysters into toasted rolls. We divided the book into three sections:

Pearls of Wisdom presents interviews with people who have special expertise in oyster issues. Their insights cover topics ranging from Chesapeake oyster history and music to cocktails and family memories.

Oyster Houses & Raw Bars profiles 120+ restaurants in the Chesapeake region, showing where to go for fresh oysters and what to order once you arrive. Many other places serve oysters, but these met our criteria, because they show a commitment to the emerging oyster scene or oysters are a central theme in their restaurant. They have dedicated shuckers, shellfish displayed in icy cases, chalkboards with daily oyster specials or menus listing multiple brands.

Chesapeake Aquafarms & Oyster Brands is an extensive list of 70+ Maryland and Virginia oyster growers and the specific brands they produce. They are categorized by a ground-breaking 13-zone system that helps you order like a pro by describing their unique flavors.

The book also includes an Oyster House & Aquafarm Index and a Taste Chart with 100+ Chesapeake oyster brands.

Meet the Authors

Bill Wade was born in Maryland and raised on Chesapeake oysters, crabs and rockfish. He is beloved by restless shuckers and feared by all-you-can-eat oyster festival hosts because of his voracious appetite for bivalves.

Susan Elnicki Wade has worked at restaurants in Pittsburgh, New York, and Washington, DC. As a water-to-table seafood enthusiast, she scours the Bay in search of new ways to prepare oysters. Her articles have appeared in *MarinaLife Magazine* and *Washingtonian Magazine*.

The Wades, who also wrote *Crab Decks & Tiki Bars of the Chesapeake Bay*, each have 20+ years experience in the publishing industry and live in Washington, DC, with their two sons and a rowdy husky.

More Oysters Online

We hope you enjoy *Chesapeake Oyster Lovers' Handbook* and its treasure trove of resources designed to demystify the ever-evolving oyster scene and lead you on exciting bivalve quests around the Bay. As you plan oyster adventures, please check our web site and Facebook page for updates, blogs and news about Chesapeake oysters.

www.weloveoysters.com

Pearls of Wisdom

Chesapeake Oyster Lovers Handbook

Pearls of Wisdom

New Oyster Cult: Celebrate
The Bay's Epic Comeback Tour
~ *by Susan Elnicki Wade*

Chesapeake Bay oysters were once the divas of the world's seafood stage. But global demand nearly decimated the Bay's oysters, so they've been playing second fiddle to New England and West Coast bivalves. Now they're back on top, ready to reclaim their place as first-class contenders.

During the oyster golden era in 1929, Cole Porter wrote a song called *The Tale of the Oyster* about a social-climbing bivalve who lounged on a silver platter among fashion queens and millionaires. The tune fit the flamboyant Gatsby era when champagne flowed at high society affairs and Chesapeake oysters were the rage. This savory delicacy was slurped down at unimaginable rates, and watermen scoured every corner of the Bay to keep up with the world's voracious appetite.

The supply seemed inexhaustible, but 50 years after Porter's song, over-harvesting, disease and pollution had annihilated the Chesapeake oyster beds. In the mid-1800s, the

Bay cranked out 20 million bushels of oysters each year. By the late 1980s, the annual total catch sunk to 20,000 bushels.

Sending Out an S.O.S.

In the 1990s, environmentalists, government officials, businessmen and watermen banded together to save the Bay. Oyster Recover Partnership returned 1,200 tons of recycled shells to the Bay to create bivalve reefs, and Chesapeake Bay Foundation planted 150 million oysters along the shores. In turn the oysters, which filter about 50 gallons of water per day, helped clean up the mess people made in their habitat. That's like drinking a keg of beer every day to make your neighborhood is a better place to live.

Slowly but surely, the Bay and its oyster population have come back. Virginia sold 654,000 oysters in 2014 — a huge jump over the 24,000 bushels harvested in 2003. And the forecast for next year is even brighter, with more than 53 million oysters expected to hit the market.

Pappa's Got a Brand New Bag

Everyone has a stake in the recovery, but aquafarmers are instrumental in changing the oyster industry. For centuries, watermen worked the Bay's bottom until it was nearly tapped out, but new aquaculture techniques offer sustainable solutions. Today's farmed oysters are grown inside  protective cages, taste as delicious as wild oysters and are

Pearls of Wisdom

harvested year-round, breaking the old rule of only eating oysters in months with the letter R.

Only about 5% of the oysters pulled from the Bay are wild — tonged or dredged in the old-fashioned method. The lion's share comes from aquafarming. Converting traditional watermen to new-age aquaculture isn't easy. The "new truck test" turns many oyster hunters into farmers, says Travis Croxton, co-owner of the Rappahannock River Oyster Co. "When a traditional waterman sees an aquafarmer driving a shiny new pick-up truck, he starts thinking that maybe farming oysters isn't such a bad idea."

Despite cleaner water and eco-friendly production methods, aquafarmers ran into snags when they first brought their wares to market. Chesapeake oysters had a tarnished image of being nearly extinct or carrying disease. To squelch market concerns, oyster aquafarmers showcased the new Chesapeake bivalve world-wide and highlighted the strict health and food safety standards they adopted.

One Species, Multiple Personalities

Nobody bellies up to a bar and asks for "a beer." You name the specific brand you want. Likewise, it helps to know what you want when ordering oysters. The Bay is home to one native species, *Crassostrea virginica,* so the region's bivalves get lumped into a group, and many think they all taste the same.

Pearls of Wisdom

But Chesapeake oysters come in a medley of flavors, depending on the salinity, temperature and food sources in the area where they're grown. From Maryland's buttery Choptank Sweets to Virginia's salty Chincoteagues, unique "merroirs" or tastes emerge from the Chesapeake waters.

To counter the one species/one taste misconception, many aquafarmers use catchy marketing to differentiate their oysters from others in the Bay and beyond. Similar to craft beer or specialty wines, witty oyster branding is intended to create memorable identities, build market loyalty and capture a sense of adventure.

Some brands use seductive names to play off oysters' legendary aphrodisiac powers. For instance, a night of nibbling on Skinny Dipper or Pleasure House oysters could lead to regrettable behavior. You might need a dozen of Maryland's Sweet Jesus oysters for morning-after redemption.

Geographic locations and animal names are favorite themes, such as Black Horse, Eagle Flats, Parrot Island and Stingray. Tough guys might be attracted to War Shore, Shooting Point or Battle Creek oysters, and it's hard for anyone to resist a cool plate of Sea-Licious Oysters.

Shucking Off Old Habits

The hot trend in today's oyster biz is "access for everyone," says Tim Devine, owner of Barren Island Oysters on Maryland's Eastern Shore. White linen and crystal glass establishments aren't going anywhere. They're part of the oyster lovers' tradition, but now you find oyster bars to fit everyone's wishes and wallets. Newcomers to the oyster scene are greeted with sample plates and tips on which to try.

Amidst the old-guard seafood houses in Washington, DC, is a new type of oyster bar, called Eat The Rich. Named after a 1980s Motörhead tune, its modern urban décor defies high-end old-school traditions with exposed brick walls, wire oyster cages dangling from the ceiling and hip music. Why heavy metal and oysters? Co-owners Derek Brown and Travis Croxton love Motörhead, metal and punk rock. "It's that simple. I only fill my bars with things I love," admits Brown. Today's oyster hunters love it too, because they want upscale cuisine in relaxed settings where jeans and T-shirts are fine.

Thanks to the resurgence of the Chesapeake oyster population, those buck-a-shuck oysters you eat in corner pubs are the same ones served on silver trays by waiters dressed in tuxedos. They're all delectable Chesapeake oysters grown in coves and rivers along the Bay by a new wave of watermen.

Chesapeake Oyster Lovers Handbook

Pearls of Wisdom

Oyster Sidekicks: Cocktails Required, Toppings Optional

*~ by Dylan Salmon,
Dylan's Oyster Cellar, Baltimore, MD*

When you belly up to an oyster bar, it's time to begin your plan of attack. Let's say the raw bar offers three different kinds of oysters that day, all harvested in local waters. You and your oyster-eating companion should try all three varieties to experience their subtle taste differences.

Here is my trick: Make sure you both sample at least two of each oyster, so you can try each one naked. That's right — in the nude (not you, but your oyster). Try each variety completely on its own devoid of sauce to truly savor the flavor profile of that specific oyster and its body of water.

Feel free to guzzle a beer or sip wine in between to cleanse your palate and explore flavor pairings. When you have a mental note of their tastes, you can play with condiments accordingly. Consider hot sauce and lemon on a sweet oyster and maybe mignonette on the salts.

The fact of the matter is oysters are supposed to be fun, celebratory and primal. Disregard rules and regulations dictating how to eat them or what to drink with them. People have their own set of preferences and traditions that guide

Pearls of Wisdom 9

them around the icy tray. So, experiment, enjoy yourself and eat a few naked. You'll be surprised just how delicious Chesapeake Bay oysters taste all by themselves.

Tantalizing Toppings
Cocktail sauce, Tabasco, lemon and mignonette are the norm, but here are condiment stand-outs you'll want to try:

- **Olive oil, salt and pepper:** Commonplace in Portugal, it's a unique garnish especially with a dry sherry.
- **Fresh grated horseradish:** When grated fresh, this is a sublime topping washed down with an earthy stout.
- **Slurp 'n Burp:** Dump six oysters, hot sauce and cocktail sauce into your pint of beer, stir it up and chug it down. Rocky would be proud.
- **Cracker sandwich:**   Put a Bay oyster on a saltine cracker, garnish as you like and top with another cracker. Great for kids and adults alike.
- **Vinegar and a slice of hard-boiled egg:** This might sound weird, but it's an old Baltimore tradition and can be pretty good if done right.
- **Drawn butter:** This is a bad idea! Cold oysters make butter congeal, which is pretty unappetizing.

What To Sip While You Slurp
When it comes to choosing beverages that best suit fresh oysters, stick with the adage, "Drink what you like." Or ask the bartender to suggest house specialty pairings that can heighten your experience, because you might get turned on to a wine, spirit or beer that you never tried before.

At Dylan's Oyster Cellar, our house cocktail is called the Gin Dandy, a light, playful drink that pairs perfectly with a cool plate of oysters. It's a play on the Gin Buck that balances the herbal gin notes with ginger and a little Campari to take down the sweetness a bit. With its strong effect, citrus and herb notes, and light refreshing finish, gin creates ideal libations for oysters in the summer months. Now that we can safely enjoy these tender bivalves year-round, it's good to have go-to cocktails when the temperatures rise.

Another one of my favorite pairings is Union Craft Brewery's Old Pro. It's a Gose-style beer, which is a German sour ale with sea salt added. For some people, it's a strange flavor, but be daring and give it a spin. You might enjoy what it does to your palate and how nicely it washes down a dozen sweet Chesapeake oysters.

In the winter months stouts and porters are king ales that rule the beer and oyster pairing world. The royal combo can hit the right flavor notes to warm you up while slurping. Also recommended is Flying Dog Brewery's Pearl Necklace Oyster Stout with a dash of oyster juice mixed in each batch.

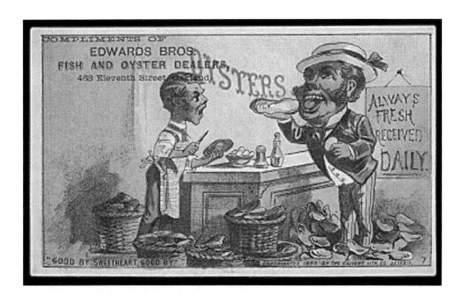

Pearls of Wisdom **11**

Discover the Harmony of Oysters & Bay Culture

*~ by Kevin "Brother Shucker" Brooks,
Eastport Oyster Boys, Annapolis, MD*

Eastport Oyster Boys love to share our passion for all things Chesapeake, especially our favorite bivalve...the *Crassostrea virginica!* As Musical Goodwill Ambassadors of the City of Annapolis and Maritime Republic of Eastport, we're often considered the "House Band of the Chesapeake."

We are inspired by the history of the oyster in the lore, culture and health of the Bay. Our songs and stories are meant to move others to follow in our wake in celebrating this unique estuary and its connection to our heritage.

The Bay's history is full of exciting tales about the hard life of watermen, the conflict between tradition and progress, and unique lifestyle of those who work, live and play on the Bay. Our music is an expression of respect for the past and a call to action to become better stewards of the Bay.

My infatuation and admiration for oysters began at an early age. My father was in the boating canvas business, and I got to see all types of vessels from Baltimore's old Inner

Harbor to the Eastern Shore. I was allowed to go with him on Saturdays and was amazed by his ability to create workable pieces of nautical art. He loved oysters, and we'd always stop at a local fish market for an oyster and crab cake treat. I was in awe as he slurped a quick dozen, washed down with a cold Natty Boh. Then he'd smile and say, "Let's go home son."

Although these memories belong to my past, they join the collective experience of Marylanders and Virginians who live on the Bay's shores and have oysters in their heart and soul. When we sing about boats and beer and bivalves, we feel the spray from the waves, and it feels like home.

Our music welcomes newcomers to the Chesapeake clan. As we perform at oyster roasts and festivals, we share tales of daily life on the water to folks from everywhere. We find a special pleasure in watching someone taste a fresh oyster for the first time or pry one open with a shucking knife. These rites of passage help them understand the spirit of Bay.

Oysters are an irreplaceable icon for the Bay, and it's impossible to separate them from its history, economy and culture. That's why they're an essential part of our band name. Sure, crabs are scrappy little buggers with a role in the imagery of the region. But oysters are more romantic and tell a deeper tale of the struggles and triumphs of the Chesapeake Bay.

Chesapeake Oyster Lovers Handbook

Baltimore & Its Oysters: A Trip down Memory Lane

~ *by Nick Schauman,*
The Local Oyster, Baltimore, MD

Oysters are an essential part of Baltimore's culinary traditions. Growing up in there in the '70s & '80s, we ate crabs in the summer and oysters all winter long. Just like the generations before us, what we ate depended on the season. The "R" month rule always applied, and I couldn't wait for September, because that's when we got our first oysters of the year.

As a kid, we took frequent trips to Lexington Market with my grandpop to get a couple dozen shucked on styrofoam plates. Almost every Sunday we had roast beef sandwiches and oyster stew while Dad and Poppsy watched the Colts on TV.

Then came the annual Cockeysville Fire Department fried oyster supper in December. My grandma and her lady friends from church would sit in her dining room and pad oyster for weeks leading up to the big event. It was always one of my favorite occasions of the season.

Every family gathering, especially Thanksgiving, we'd set up a makeshift oyster bar in our garage. To stock it, we'd

Pearls of Wisdom

drive up Pulaski Highway looking for the plywood sign that said "Oysters for Sale." We'd taste one before purchasing a wooden bushel full, straight from the back of a pickup truck. No refrigeration needed, because it was always cold in November. The oysters were big and briny and fresh from the Bay. Once we got them home, we'd turn on the space heater and transistor radio, lay a kitchen towel on the workbench, and Grandpop, Dad and I shucked oysters all day until they were gone. Grandma even opened a few with her can opener. That's how we did it, and that's why I love oysters so much.

Today things are different. Pickup trucks full of oysters no longer idle on the side of the road. No one I know has heard of a padded oyster. With hundreds of oyster farms up and down the East Coast harvesting bivalves year-round, the "R" month rule no longer applies. The one constant in Baltimore that remains the same is people still love oysters.

It's hard to explain the reason why, but oysters just make you feel good. Three years ago when I started The Local Oyster, Baltimore's first traveling oyster bar, I wanted to remind people of how things used to be. Now I am the owner of a raw bar just a few blocks away from Lexington Market, the place where I ate my first oyster. Hopefully, The Local Oyster helps Baltimore hold dear our culinary traditions whenever we slurp down a perfectly shucked, ice-cold, farm-raised oyster off a compostable plate.

Chesapeake Oyster Lovers Handbook

Chesapeake Bay Oyster Houses & Restaurants

Chesapeake Oyster Lovers Handbook

Baltimore

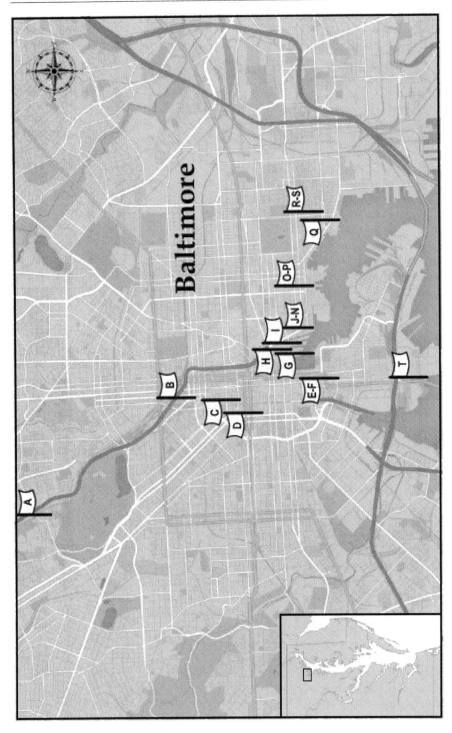

Baltimore

- Ⓐ Woodberry Kitchen 18
- Ⓑ Ryleigh's Oyster Mount Vernon 20
- Ⓒ The Local Oyster 22
- Ⓓ John W. Faidley Seafood 24
- Ⓔ Ryleigh's Oyster Federal Hill 26
- Ⓕ Nick's Oyster Bar 28
- Ⓖ Rusty Scupper 30
- Ⓗ Phillips Seafood Baltimore 32
- Ⓘ McCormick & Schmick's Baltimore Inner Harbor 34
- Ⓙ Apropoe's 36
- Ⓚ Wit & Wisdom 38
- Ⓛ Oceanaire Seafood Room Baltimore 40
- Ⓜ Heavy Seas Alehouse Baltimore 42
- Ⓝ Mussel Bar & Grille Baltimore 44
- Ⓞ Riptide by the Bay 46
- Ⓟ Thames Street Oyster House 48
- Ⓠ BoatHouse Canton 50
- Ⓡ Mama's on the Half Shell 52
- Ⓢ Plug Ugly's Publick House 54
- Ⓣ Nick's Fish House 56

Woodberry Kitchen

2010 Clipper Park Road
Baltimore, MD 21211
(410) 464-8000
www.woodberrykitchen.com

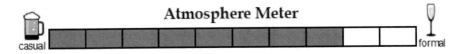

Atmosphere Meter — casual / formal

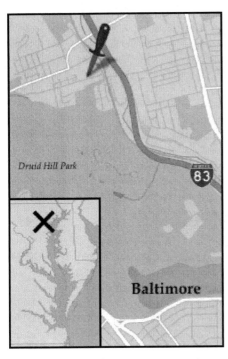

Woodbury Kitchen is a world-class restaurant in a magnificent place that represents Baltimore's remarkable past and future.

It's located in historic Clipper Mill Industrial Park, which was a manufacturing powerhouse for nearly 150 years. At its peak, 11 mills operated here producing textiles that were sewn into sails in World War I, cast iron columns for the U.S. capitol dome, and engines that were used around the globe. A massive fire in 1995 devastated what was once America's largest machine plant.

From the ashes, a modern community has risen. In the ruins of elegant 19th century industrial buildings, a vibrant neighborhood bustles with artisans, glassblowers, galleries, a brewery and more on the way. Woodberry Kitchen's spacious stone and brick building was constructed in 1870 and used for casting iron and steel. The gigantic industrial smelting furnaces have been removed and replaced with wood-burning stoves that cook fine Chesapeake seafood.

The chef is an advocate of locally grown, organic and sustainable ingredients that elevate traditional Bay cuisine to create a fresh contemporary dining experience. Local oysters from aquafarms in Maryland, Virginia and the Atlantic seaboard come shucked on the half shell or fried to a perfect crisp with fish pepper mayo and herbs. Middleneck clams are simmered with buckwheat noodles, and the invasive blue catfish is blackened and served with heirloom grits. Rockfish is pulled from the oven with smoked oyster chowder.

The menu follows the harvests of the season, but this place is a wonderful destination whether the temperature is balmy or blustery. Graceful arched windows invite sunshine indoors to brighten rustic wood furniture in the dining rooms. Reams of chopped wood are stacked along the walls. Delicate white lights strung above the outdoor patio create a magical glow on summer nights.

Baltimore

Ryleigh's Oyster Mount Vernon

1225 Cathedral Street
Baltimore, MD 21201
(410) 539-2093
www.ryleighs.com

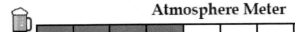

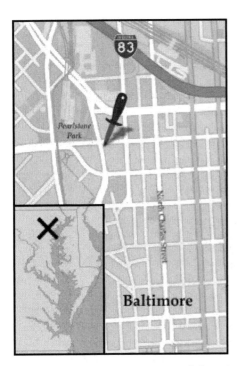

Ryleigh's Oyster Mount Vernon is surrounded by organizations that enrich society. Meyerhoff Symphony Orchestra is across the street, and the Art Institute, University of Baltimore and Lyric Opera House are just a block away. Even Representative Elijah Cummings maintains an office around the corner.

This oyster house contributes to the greater good by providing a lovely gathering place for everyone who comes to these honorable institutions and fancies fresh regional oysters.

The décor inside this splendid 19th century red brick building reflects a reverence for Chesapeake bivalves. Above the front entrance hangs a chandelier made from a metal aquafarm cage with shells and sparkling lights inside. Every piece of art projects an oyster theme: photos of boats, watermen's tongs, maps where North American oysters are grown and dramatic bivalve quotes from literary figures such as Jonathan Swift and Shakespeare.

An icy oyster station is laid into the bar, and a chalkboard with daily bivalve specials hangs upon the wall. During a recent visit, Shooting Points and Nassawadox Salts (VA), Blue Points (CT), and Salt Ponds and Malpeques (PEI) got shucked. Avery's Pearls are exclusively grown for the restaurant near Hog Island, VA. Happy hour buck-a-shucks make sure everyone, from students to cellists, can afford a bite of bivalve. Whether dining outside on the patio or being content to stay indoors, you encounter a medley of Chesapeake seafood on the menu. Highlights include oysters char-grilled with garlic butter, steamed Maine mussels and Hog Island clams, Eastern Shore-style crab cakes, and shrimp with creamy grits. Steaks, blackened chicken and juicy burgers are also available.

Baltimore

The Local Oyster

520 Park Avenue
Baltimore, MD 21201
(410) 371-6853
www.thelocaloyster.com

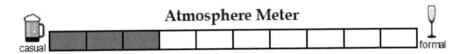

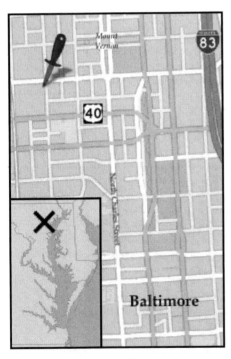

The Local Oyster is right across the avenue from the Maryland Historical Society, a valuable archive for bivalve enthusiasts to dig up articles and prints on the regional oyster trade. When you are finished reading and feel an irresistible urge for eating oysters, head over to the sunny side of the street.

Inside Mount Vernon Marketplace among vendors selling baked goods, Asian dumplings and other delightful sundries, you discover one of Baltimore's newest hot spots for cool oysters. It's a casual contemporary place with freshly painted white walls and vintage oyster cans arranged around the specials board. The vibe is energetic fun.

The glass-enclosed oyster station hosts an impressive inventory of local bivalves. Signs heralding their brand names

Chesapeake Oyster Lovers' Handbook

Baltimore

are held in upright shucking knives. During a recent visit, the amiable shucker suggested a taste tour of the Chesapeake Bay and beyond, sampling Skinny Dipper and Huckleberry from Maryland, White Stone from Virginia, Salt Grass Point from Prince Edward Island, and North Star from Rhode Island.

   Hot out of the roaster come oysters topped with Old Bay, butter and parmesan cheese. Littleneck clams arrive bubbling with ham, butter and parmesan. Savory crab soup contains the spicy secrets of a family recipe, and chilled shrimp salad tastes like seaside freshness tucked inside a toasty bun.

   In addition to this terrific location, The Local Oyster can bring the bivalves to you. The owner, a Baltimore shellebrity renown for his unbridled warmth and flawless shucking speed, can help arrange events at your home or other venues to create an oyster extravaganza for your friends.

John W. Faidley Seafood

203 North Paca Street
Baltimore, MD 21201
(410) 727-4898
www.faidleyscrabcakes.com

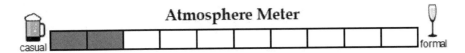

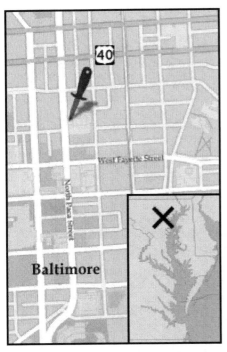

Faidley Seafood began in 1886, and four generations of the family-owned restaurant have worked in this iconic Baltimore site. It's housed inside Lexington Market, which has been around since 1782 and is America's oldest market. When you come for oysters, you also experience a slice of local history.

In the market, nearly 100 vendors display every imaginable type of seafood tightly packed in ice. And it's the only destination in this book that sells muskrat, raccoon and alligator when they're in season. It's noisy, often crowded and filled with a unique cast of characters, but you can't beat its old-school unpretentious charm.

Faidley's oyster bar is in the center of the action. A sign above the shuckers proclaims they serve over 1 million oysters

Baltimore  **25**

and clams each year. They arrive on white Styrofoam plates with a squirt of cocktail sauce. Beer comes in plastic cups. But modest table settings don't matter much when the oysters are harvested out of the sweetest spots along the Bay from Hoopers Island to Chincoteague Bay and the Choptank River.

The restaurant's fist-sized, no-filler Maryland crab cakes regularly win awards, and crab soup comes in red and white varieties. Cooks stick to home-style Chesapeake fare featuring some of the freshest catch in town. Oysters come in bowls of creamy stew or deep fried in baskets. Jumbo shrimp are stuffed with backfin crab meat, and the seafood gumbo harbors enough heat to ward off a wintery chill. It's easy to fill up on Southern-influenced side dishes, such as pickled beets, cucumber salad, collard greens and fried corn on the cob dusted with Old Bay. But your sweet tooth will be grateful if you save room for Berger's Cookies as dessert.

Baltimore

Ryleigh's Oyster Federal Hill

36 East Cross Street
Baltimore, MD 21230
(410) 539-2093
www.ryleighs.com

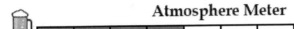 Atmosphere Meter

The sign out front with a three-foot tall super-oyster mounted in the middle says that Ryleigh's Oyster Federal Hill is serious about bivalves. When you walk around the restaurant admiring exposed brick walls covered with oyster art, fishnets and artifacts of Chesapeake life on the water, you're certain it's a genuine oyster haven.

On the left past the outdoor patio stands a shucking station with bivalves blanketed in ice and small wooden sticks identifying various local aquafarm brands. Avery's Pearl is the most noteworthy of the bunch. The oyster is grown exclusively for the eatery in Hog Island, VA, and is named after the owner's daughter. During a recent trip, the list oysters on ice sounded like a bivalve lover's Top Ten Hits of the East Coast including Shooting Point and Nassawadox Salt

Chesapeake Oyster Lovers' Handbook

Baltimore

(VA), Blue Point (CT), Salt Pond (RI), Raspberry Point and Malpeque (Prince Edward Island), Caraquet (New Brunswick) and Katama Bay (MA).

To make Ryleigh's even more appealing to bivalve seekers, the restaurant offers $1 buck-a-shuck discounts at happy hour and hosts the annual Moet Champagne Oyster Ball, a fundraiser that donates proceeds to charities such as Oyster Recover Partnership and the Living Classroom's program to restore a skipjack dating back to 1911.

Established in 2002, this Ryleigh's Oyster location is the original, which spawned sister restaurants in Mount Vernon and Hunt Valley. They all have a casual atmosphere and exceptional seafood. Standouts from this kitchen include char-grilled oysters topped with garlic butter, fried oyster spinach cobb salad, True Blue Maryland crab cakes, steamed Maine mussels and Hog Island clams. Burger and blackened chicken sandwiches welcome hungry landlubbers.

Nick's Oyster Bar

1065 South Charles Street
Baltimore, MD 21230
(410) 685-2020
www.nicksoysterbar.com

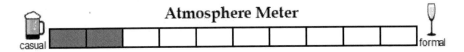

Atmosphere Meter: casual — formal

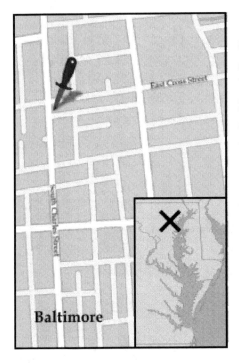

Baltimore

The legendary Cross Street Market runs an entire city block on Federal Hill between Light and Charles Streets. Since the mid-19th century, vendors have presented a menagerie of seafood, meats, sausages, produce, flowers and even chocolates shaped like crabs.

Nick's opened inside this Baltimore landmark in 1972 offering a place to sit down for a beer and a bivalve after strolling through the market. It's not fancy, but it's fun.

Without many windows to let in natural light, the place is illuminated by neon beer signs and a backlit stained glass of colorful fish. From corrugated metal awnings below the ceiling hang Ravens banners and handwritten signs for daily specials and fresh catch delivered by local watermen. Tall stools line up along the raw bar, and weathered wooden barrels double as tables. The atmosphere is busy and boisterous, heightened by a turbulent sea of purple and black jerseys during football season when the Steelers challenge the hometown team.

Behind her glass case, the shucker is in constant motion filling customers' half shell orders on paper plates. She patiently opens three types of oysters: Blue Points from Connecticut, Chincoteagues from Virginia and a rotation of wild and farmed Maryland bivalves that changes daily. Crisp fried oysters cruise to the table, along with award-winning crab cakes that have been featured on TV shows. Maryland crab soup is spiced to meet traditional Bay standards.

The first sushi bar in the area stands next to the oyster bar rolling slivers of fresh catch in rice and thin seaweed sheets. The rest of the menu features local seafood fried or steamed. Mussels, clams, rockfish and shrimp are among the favorites.

Rusty Scupper

402 Key Highway
Baltimore, MD 21230
(410) 727-3678
www.rusty-scupper.com

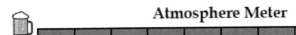

Oyster lovers who appreciate a panoramic view of Baltimore's city skyline should come to the harbor waterfront and climb to the third story upper deck at Rusty Scupper. Located at the base of Federal Hill, it's arguably one of the best vantage points in town.

The raw bar serves three brands of oysters that encourage taste tests to experience a full spectrum of flavors from sweet to salty. Order a few of each type and witness the taste of the ocean unfold. Canadian Gigamoto oysters have a mild fruity flavor with a buttery finish, Maryland's Choptank Sweets carry a hint of salt with a sweet crisp ending, and Delaware Bay's bivalves are plump with a distinctly briny tint. Once you complete the delectable circuit, you'll never go back to one-brand platters of oysters again.

The raw bar presents other chilled favorites such as jumbo shrimp and blue crab claw cocktails. The menu swims with treasures from the sea: seared ahi tuna, grilled rockfish, blackened diver scallops and Caribbean mahi mahi. Beef, chicken and burgers accommodate meat eaters.

The atmosphere is contemporary and comfortable, with subtle nautical artwork and exposed wood rafters softening the décor. A photo gallery of local celebrities, sports figures and politicians line the hallway. Rusty Scupper is owned by Select Restaurants from Cleveland, but it fortifies ties to the Bay by purchasing fresh catch from local watermen. As a good neighbor, it also joined Oyster Recovery Partnership (ORP), an alliance of regional restaurants that donate used oyster shells for recycling. As a result, ORP collects thousands of used shells every year and plants millions of baby oysters in the Bay to help replenish the population.

Phillips Seafood Baltimore

601 East Pratt Street
Baltimore, MD 21202
(410) 685-6600
www.phillipsseafood.com

Atmosphere Meter

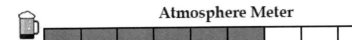

casual — formal

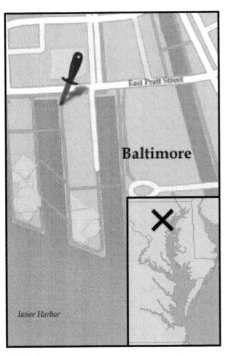

Everybody thinks Phillips equals crabs. That's true, but the secret to success and longevity for this iconic Maryland restaurant is building on its brand and offering what its diners like.

Right now, people all around the Bay are gobbling up oysters, so Phillips decided to go with the flow and shore up its raw bar. Blue Points are regulars on the menu, and Chesapeake oysters from Maryland and Virginia are rotated weekly to showcase local bivalves. Clams on the half shell and shrimp cocktail are also presented on ice. Clams casino and mussels steamed with garlic and white wine butter underscore the new mollusk manifesto. Excellent crab cakes are a slam dunk here, along with classics such as fried oysters, broiled seafood platters, seared scallops, clam bakes and flounder stuffed with jumbo lump crab.

Phillips recently expanded the outdoor patio and built a large wooden crab deck with picnic tables that extends out above the water. Inside renovations aim to shrink the lines of people waiting for an Eastern Shore seafood feast. They remodeled the piano bar area and dining rooms to provide additional seating. The refurbished spaces have a fresh clean look and a more inviting atmosphere.

This is not the first time Phillips has shifted plans to serve Baltimore better. Back in the 1960s, the Inner Harbor was surrounded by run-down warehouses and dilapidated buildings. Mayor William Donald Shaefer and local developers envisioned a rebirth of the harbor with shiny skyscrapers, a convention center and world-class aquarium. When Shaefer sought an anchor restaurant to attract locals and tourists, the Phillips family answered his call and opened their Harborplace restaurant in 1980, long before others were willing to take the risk.

McCormick & Schmick's Baltimore Inner Harbor

711 Eastern Avenue
Baltimore, MD 21202
(410) 234-1300
www.mccormickandschmicks.com

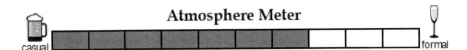

Atmosphere Meter

casual — formal

McCormick & Schmick's outdoor patio presents a glorious view of Baltimore's dynamic waterfront. But a few steps away is a sight that every oyster adventurer should see — the Seven Foot Knoll Lighthouse.

Built in 1855, it's the oldest screwpile lighthouse in Maryland. Uniquely designed for the Chesapeake Bay, scores of these warning beacons once stood on the shoreline to warn oystermen and seafaring captains of dangerous waters. Only a handful of them remain today. The well-preserved lighthouse was moved to Pier 5 from the mouth of the Patapsco River in 1988 as part of the Baltimore Maritime Museum.

Baltimore

After you explore the historic lighthouse, McCormick & Schmick's offers a pleasant setting for reflecting on the Bay's maritime traditions and enjoying a tray of fresh-shucked oysters. Connecticut Blue Points, Maryland Choptank Sweets and Virginia James River oysters are standard raw bar fare, along with oysters Rockefeller and oysters Kilpatrick with bacon, Worcestershire and Tabasco sauces. Other regional bivalves are shucked, depending on the season. Bay seafood favorites include jumbo crab cakes, grilled rockfish and steamed mussels. Fish dishes from around the globe range from Atlantic salmon to yellowfin tuna.

Since 1998, this M&S location has delivered fresh catch in a warm upscale environment. Stools with black leather seats are stationed along the wooden bar and stained glass lights overhead create an old, established feeling. Pictures of oysters, sailboats and ocean creatures garnish dark wood paneling on the walls. The open galley kitchen shows how smoothly meals move from grill to tabletop.

Chesapeake Oyster Lovers' Handbook

Baltimore

Apropoe's

700 Aliceanna Street
Baltimore, MD 21202
(410) 895-1879
www.apropoesharboreast.com

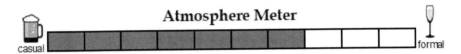

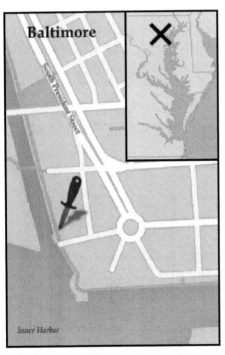

Bourbon matched with oysters creates fascinating yet unconventional pairings. So, Apropoe's encourages guests to be daring and craft new flavor adventures with its list of almost 50 different bourbons, whiskeys, ryes and scotches that run the gamut from Angels Envy to Whistle Pig Rye.

When coupled with a Chesapeake Bay challenge, you can decide if you prefer briny bivalves with bitters or buttery ones with oaky liquors on the rocks. An impressive inventory of wine, craft beers and bubbly opens up a world of possibilities. During the week, only a few oyster brands are on ice, but the chef ups the ante on weekends with an array of regional bivalves. Choptank Sweets and Skinny Dippers from Maryland and Rappahannocks from Virginia often make the grade.

Baltimore **37**

The menu adds a touch of Baltimore to modern American pub fare, with fresh ingredients and herbs plucked from the hotel rooftop garden. Smoked corn adds zest and texture to Maryland crab chowder, and New England lobster rolls meet Chesapeake spice with a touch of Old Bay aioli. Noteworthy seafood dishes include plump crab cakes, pan-roasted diver scallops and grilled swordfish. Salads, sandwiches, burgers, steak, chicken and pork round out the dining options.

Located in the Baltimore Marriott Waterfront Hotel, this spacious restaurant marks the border of Harbor East, which lies between the Inner Harbor and Fells Point. Planning for this area started back in the 1980s when city officials wanted to convert old industrial warehouses into a new urban destination with a lively waterfront promenade. This growing neighborhood is packed with luxury hotels, restaurants, shops, office buildings and high-end condos.

Apropoe's décor has a sophisticated contemporary design with subtle lighting and exposed brick walls. The large dining room is divided into small privacy areas with sheer black screens. Lounges with comfortable couches flank the bar area, and tall windows overlook the Pier 6 Pavilion music venue.

Wit & Wisdom

200 International Drive
Baltimore, MD 21202
(410) 576-5800
www.witandwisdombaltimore.com

Atmosphere Meter

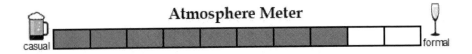

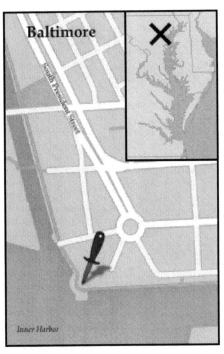

When Wit & Wisdom opened in 2012 at Four Seasons Hotel, oyster lovers in Harbor East applauded the arrival of a place that elevates dining experiences by appealing to all the senses. The instant you step inside, a sweet smoky aroma sparks your sense of smell and lures you into ordering dishes from a wood-burning oven. The sound of harbor waves on a waterfront patio and laughter from the bar show that seaside restaurants generate a special tone.

The décor is visually pleasing and contemporary. The dining room is divided by open shelves stacked to the rafters with candles that cast a warm glow on dark wooden floors and comfy brown leather seats. But eyes grow wide with excitement when bivalve fans see the raw bar offerings.

A long list of chilled treats presents fresh seafood from the Eastern seaboard. Local oysters include Battle Creek, War Shore, Olde Salt, Stingray and HongaTonk. Other regional bivalves float in often depending on the season. Littleneck clams on the half shell and citrus-steamed razor clams try to outshine shellfish gems such as blue crab cocktail, mesquite-smoked mussels and scallop ceviche.

The dinner menu takes a modern twist on the cultural heritage of Baltimore and the Bay's Eastern Shore. Standout starters: grilled Chesapeake rockfish, crab bisque with black garlic buttered toast and seared scallops sprinkled with crispy chicken skin. Crab cakes meet the tough local standards, and Virginia swordfish is grilled to perfection. Meat eaters are well served with dishes such as wood oven roasted chicken, Catoctin Mountain Farm pork trio, New York strip steaks and Gunpowder bison fillet with red wine reduction.

Oceanaire Seafood Room Baltimore

801 Aliceanna Street
Baltimore, MD 21202
(410) 872-0000
www.theoceanaire.com

Atmosphere Meter

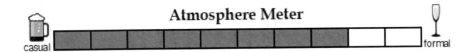
casual — formal

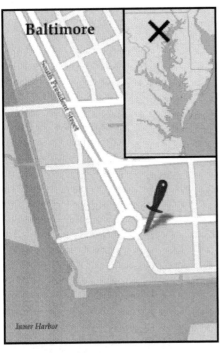

Engraved on the dining room wall is the famous quote, "To eat an oyster is to kiss the sea on its lips." It's the first clue that Oceanaire is wild about oysters.

In the center of the bar area, you spot a great glass-enclosed case filled with ice and oysters, manned by shuckers at the ready to assemble half shells on silver platters. And you'll be hooked on this elegant seafood house once you hear about the autumn Oyster Bash that celebrates local bivalves with craft beer, wine pairings and live music.

The oyster bar kicks off with Chesapeake favorites: Skinny Dippers (MD) and Pungoteagues and Battle Creeks (VA). Then it rolls out an inventory of East Coast darlings, such as

Purple Mountain-Hood Canals (WA), Raspberry Points (PEI), and Whalebacks (ME). The Chilled Shellfish Platter presents a regal display of king crab legs, shrimp, lobster, mussels and oysters that would make Poseidon proud.

Entrée selections concentrate on sustainably caught Atlantic seafood prepared with regional flare and ingredients. Maryland-style crab cakes, seafood bouillabaisse and shrimp scampi on angel hair pasta are worthy of the captain's table. Only a few dishes target meat eaters: steak, chicken and pork.

For nearly a decade, Oceanaire has delivered fresh catch to Harbor East in an upscale setting. The prices are a bit steep, but the chefs guarantee high-quality seafood in an elegant dining room that's ideal for special occasions or nights to remember. The décor is modeled after a 1930s luxury cruise liner with plush red leather booths, round porthole windows and art deco light fixtures above tables with white linen cloths and polished silverware. Mounted marlins and other trophy fish are placed artfully on cream-colored walls.

Baltimore

Heavy Seas Alehouse

1300 Bank Street
Baltimore, MD 21231
(410) 753-1403
www.heavyseasalehouse.com

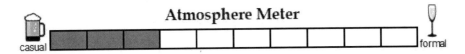

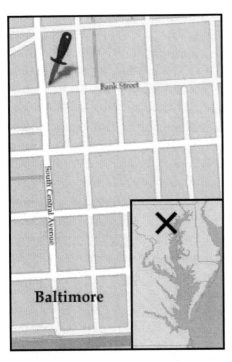

Did pirates eat oysters? Certainly. On long voyages they'd deplete their barrels of biscuits, salted beef and dried fruit, then turn to the ocean's bounty for stews of boiled fish and bivalves. After a good run of pillaging, pirates would cash in their treasure for doubloons and head to the nearest port for raucous nights of ale, oysters and maidens.

Heavy Seas Alehouse is just the kind of tavern they'd seek, welcomed by the skull and crossbones sign in front. Today's buccaneers can tap into the swashbuckler's spirit at Baltimore's locally owned craft brewery and down mugs of Heavy Seas Cutlass Amber, Loose Cannon American Hops or Peg Leg Imperial Stout. On the walls hang chalkboards that announce seasonal specialty brews and daily local oysters.

During a recent visit War Shore and Tipper's Cove oysters awaited on the half shell, but the bar wench noted that various brands from around the Chesapeake are rotated on a regular basis to keep scalawags coming back for more. Cornmeal crusted fried oysters come with pickle remoulade, and PEI mussels are steamed in Golden Ale and Old Bay broth. Seafood dishes are listed with recommended beer pairings. Mahi mahi goes well with Cross Bones Session IPA, and fish and chips are best washed down with Powder Monkey Pale Ale. Meat dishes, such as burgers, chicken and lamb, help deter hungry pirates from plundering nearby villages.

The restaurant's dining room feels like a modern interpretation of an old seafaring vessel, with thick wooden beams overhead and black benches pushed up against brick walls. The atmosphere is vibrant and welcoming. Restless guests can wander back to addition rooms with dartboards, an outdoor smoking patio and a cigar room. Note: A second location recently dropped anchor in Arlington, VA.

Mussel Bar & Grille Baltimore

1350 Lancaster Street
Baltimore, MD 21231
(410) 946-6726
www.musselbar.com

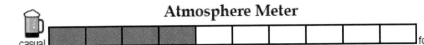

Atmosphere Meter

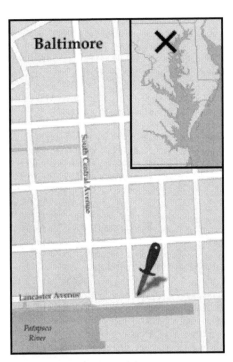

A glass and metal case embedded in the middle of the bar is the centerpiece for Mussel Bar & Grill Baltimore. Oysters recline near the bottom. Green parsley sprigs and lemon slices are arranged strategically inside to give it greater aesthetic appeal. The garnishes are not necessary, because the display is a vision of beauty to oyster lovers.

Above the shiny case hangs a chalkboard with a tantalizing list of Maryland oysters: Barren Island, Holy Grail, Chesapeake Gold and Sweet Jesus, plus Katama Bay from Massachusetts for good measure. That's when it's clear this place is about more than mussels. Same goes for its sister restaurants in Bethesda, MD, and Arlington, VA. The concept for this trinity of bistros stems from youthful memories of when the owner explored roadside dives outside Brussels with fellow chefs. His goal is to share those pleasant experiences with Americans through fine food and good Belgian beer.

Mussels, oysters and other tasty mollusks set the mood for the menu. Shuckers unveil a cool collection of chilled middle neck clams, Gulf shrimp, poached lobsters and oysters at the raw bar. The namesake mussels are prepared to order five different ways with a gamut of savory ingredients from white wine to green curry and creamy garlic. All of them come with classic frites, sweet potato fries or warm bread for dipping. Other seafood dishes include oven roasted brook trout, Maine lobster mac and cheese, and grilled ahi tuna niçoise. Chicken, lamb meatballs, braised short ribs are on hand for carnivores.

The décor is industrial chic with a lofty ceiling painted black and metal pipes stretched out between the rafters. Overstuffed leather couches and breezy curtains in the lounge create a relaxed setting for kicking back after a tough day at the office. The easy-going vibe is contagious.

Riptide by the Bay

1718 Thames Street
Baltimore, MD 21231
(410) 732-3474
www.riptidebythebay.net

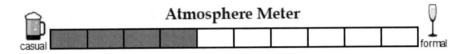

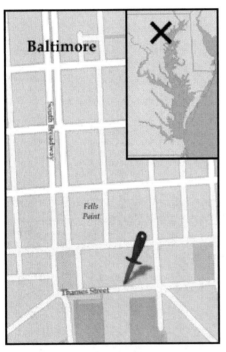

Riptide by the Bay is well known as a neighborhood pub with award-winning steamed crabs, but one of the best kept secrets in Fells Point is this place also does a fantastic job with oysters.

The chef generally offers a half dozen daily. During a recent visit, two came from Chesapeake aquafarms – Chincoteague and HongaTonk. The other three were wild caught on the Patuxent, Chester and Wye rivers. Some say the wild ones taste better, because they grow freely in their natural environment rather than piled up in cages or on ropes. Only a thorough taste test will tell, but both kinds hit the spot when oyster urges arise.

Riptide supports bivalve bingeing on Thursdays with $1 buck-a-shucks and $4 oyster shooters. Alaskan snow crab legs and peel-and-eat shrimp also grace the raw bar. The regular menu is flush with seafood, including pan-seared scallops, crab cakes, linguine with clams or shrimp, fish tacos, and lobster ravioli. Steaks, burgers, chicken and sandwiches are available for guests who prefer meat at their meals.

The restaurant is located in a charming red brick row house with a waterfront patio overlooking the harbor. Inside the dining area, wooden booths and colorfully painted walls showcase pictures of Chesapeake schooners, lighthouses, sea creatures and nautical artifacts.

The décor harkens back to the oyster bonanza of the 1800s when seafood processing and ship building jobs attracted men from around the globe. A Wild West boom time ensued with saloons and brothels crowding the docks. Gunfights erupted between Maryland and Virginia crews competing for oyster beds.

Dredging oysters was rough work, and many men didn't want to do it, especially in the frigid winter season. But sea captains needed able hands on ships, so they'd scour local taverns for recruits. Often targeting new immigrants, captains got men drunk, dragged them to the docks and shanghaied them to toil on oyster boats. The lucky ones got paid, but many were tossed overboard without ever receiving a penny.

Baltimore

Thames Street Oyster House

1728 Thames Street
Baltimore, MD 21231
(443) 449-7726
www.thamesstreetoysterhouse.com

Atmosphere Meter
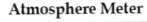

casual — formal

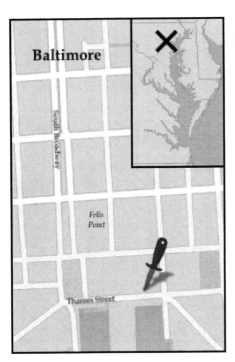

The small dark shucking station at the front of the bar does not prepare you for Thames Street's extensive raw bar. It appears that only a few are offered, but this place exceeds oyster lovers' greatest expectations.

The daily — sometimes hourly — raw bar list is held in vintage oyster cans and is laid out sushi-style on a chart with brand name, state, price and flavor description. The staff is so excited about the oyster stockpile that they trump standard chalkboard presentations by painting bivalve names on a huge antique mirror. At a recent visit, 15 oysters from the Bay, Canada, and East and West Coasts included local brands such as War Shore and Happy Oyster (VA) and Chesapeake Wild (MD). Clams, shrimp, crab claws and lobster tails were also reclining on ice.

If you can pull yourself away from the raw bar, you discover a menu that is inundated with fresh, sustainable and award-winning seafood. Fried oysters, braised mussels and lobster mac and cheese start the appetizer choices. Must-try entrees include cast iron Chesapeake crab cakes, seafood bouillabaisse, Old Bay shrimp salad roll and North Atlantic wolffish with house-made gnocchi. The number of meat dishes pales in comparison to seafood, but you leave fulfilled after a plate of burgers, steaks, pork or duck.

Located in the heart of Fells Point, this beautiful seafood restaurant offers a sweet waterfront view from the outdoor patio. The bar of this narrow turn-of-the-century rowhouse can get crowded, but a dining room upstairs helps alleviate the shoulder-to-shoulder crunch.

Understated sophisticated décor features rich woodwork, cream-colored walls, vintage light fixtures and a few paintings of sea creatures and ocean life. The atmosphere is electric, and the place is always jumping with people who are thrilled to find such a marvelous destination for slurping oysters.

BoatHouse Canton

2809 Boston Street
Baltimore, MD 21224
(410) 773-9795
www.boathousecanton.com

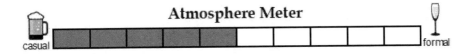

Atmosphere Meter — casual / formal

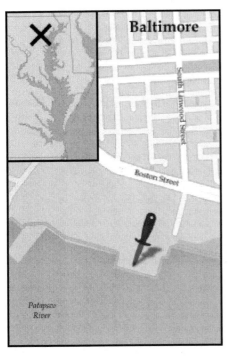

The factory smokestack and distinctive brick building that houses BoatHouse Canton stand as monuments to Baltimore's industrial history. Built around 1914, they were part of the Tin Decorating Co., or Tindeco, which manufactured colorful tin containers for cigarettes, cookies, candies, medicine, beer and talcum powder. At peak production, its 3,000 workers cranked out nearly 4 million tins a day.

The mighty machinery has been replaced with ovens and grills that churn out fine seafood by the waterfront. The location has also evolved into an oyster-eating refuge. Happy hour buck-a-shuck presents bivalves such as Rocky Shore (PEI) and James River (VA). The impressive raw bar catalog includes Choptank Sweets and Skinny Dippers from Maryland, Chincoteague Salts and

Chunus from Virginia, and Malpeques from Canada's Prince Edward Island. Steamed littleneck clams, Old Bay shrimp and mussels sautéed three ways bring smiles to the faces of mollusk fans.

Fresh catch combined with upscale pub grub guides the menu. Fried oysters and calamari deliver a crispy crunch, while the East Coast teams up with the West Coast to deliver crab cakes and Baja fish tacos. Featured entrees include sesame grilled ahi tuna steak and Atlantic pan-seared salmon. Carnivores gladly take a fork to steaks, Chesapeake chicken and turkey meatball sliders.

The newly renovated restaurant sports a contemporary décor that resembles a classic boathouse. Exposed brick walls, vaulted ceilings and beautiful arched windows surround wood tables with black metal legs. On a warm summer evening, it's hard to resist sitting on the expansive outdoor deck and relishing a spectacular view of the water.

Baltimore

Mama's on the Half Shell

2901 O' Donnell Street
Baltimore, MD 21224
(410) 276-3160
www.mamasmd.com/MamasSite

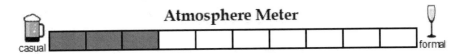

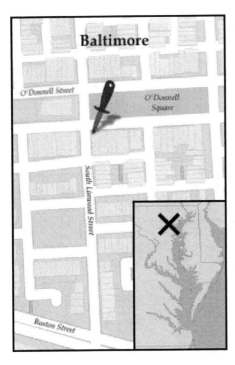

Looking for a classic Bawlmer oyster house, hon? Then head over to Canton Square and look for a sassy little mermaid wrapping her tail around the sign for Mama's on the Half Shell.

The restaurant is located in a gorgeous turn-of-the-century brick building with flowers cascading down the sides from window boxes. A black awning hovers above the patio, shading diners from the sun while they watch neighbors chitchat in the park.

The interior sports an 1800s saloon feel with a narrow bar on the left and dining room on the right. Vintage light fixtures and lovely woodwork underscore an authentic old-fashioned décor. Pictures of past and present Baltimore landmarks and legends garnish the walls. Antique oyster cans on display above the bar and porcelain oyster plates in a protective glass case confirm that the cooks prepare dishes in the traditional way that made this town famous for seafood.

Oysters dominate the raw bar on the half shell, steamed or in shooters. The house specialty shooter, Blue on Blue, tucks an oyster and cocktail sauce under four ounces of Pabst Blue Ribbon Beer. Shrimp, mussels and clams add to the bounty. During a recent visit, five brands of oysters with flavor descriptions were on tap: Madhouse (MD), Blue Point (NY), Taunton Bay (ME), Chincoteague (VA) and Salt Pond (RI).

Oysters are grilled three ways, with smoked paprika butter, applewood bacon BBQ sauce or parmesan herb sauce. Oysters are prepared in every possible fashion including Rockefeller, fried, in stews or nestled in po' boys. The rest of the menu features local seafood, crab cakes, shrimp and scallops but also offers tasty meat options such as bleu cheese crusted steaks, baby back ribs, burgers and grilled chicken.

Plug Ugly's Publick House

2908 O'Donnell Street
Baltimore, MD 21224
(410) 563-8459
www.pluguglyspub.com

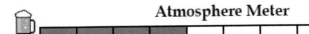

Atmosphere Meter

casual | formal

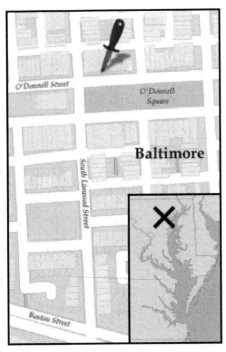

An unusual name like Plug Ugly's is sure to arouse an oyster adventurer's curiosity. So, as you wait for the shucker to open a dozen on the half shell, ask the bartender to tell the tale of this old rowhouse tavern.

It's located on Canton Square, an area that was settled in the 1800s by Irish, Polish, German and other European immigrants who worked in the factories and canneries. The Plug Uglies were a political club that operated more like a street gang in the mid-19th century. Their close ties to volunteer firehouses made the hooligans useful to corrupt politicians who wanted to control the polls on election days. As part of a plan to intimidate local voters from casting their ballots, the Plug Uglies allegedly kidnapped Edgar Allen Poe and contributed to his untimely death shortly after.

Baltimore

A good restaurant back story seems to make oysters taste even sweeter, and this fine-looking tavern has plenty of lore to enjoy while nibbling on bivalves. The raw bar list usually features a half dozen brands. During a recent visit, Skinny Dippers and Huckleberrys from southern Maryland, Olde Salts from Chincoteague, VA, and Blue Points from Connecticut were written on the chalkboard.

Eating good food is a pleasure in a place that shows a slice of life nearly 150 years ago. The pressed tin roof, long front bar, vintage light fixtures and intricate woodwork let your imagination soar back to a Chesapeake golden era. Oysters Rockefeller and parmesan-crusted scallops wrapped in prosciutto encourage bivalve beginnings, and crab and corn fritters come with Old Bay aioli. Noteworthy fishy dishes include steamer pots, fish and chips, and seafood pot pie with lobster, shrimp, scallops and crab baked in a puff pastry. Steaks, burgers, chicken and pork are also available.

Nick's Fish House

2600 Insulator Drive
Baltimore, MD 21230
(410) 347-4123
www.nicksfishhouse.com

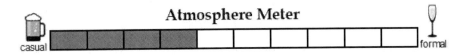

Nick's is the kind of place that rolls with the flow of the season. Ravens fans suit up in the fall, Orioles devotees are on deck in the spring, and hot Maryland crabs get picked in between.

Oysters are a year-round constant that connect the changing times of year, so they take center stage inside. Every day a large wooden display station gets filled with at least a half dozen brands of Bay bivalves. Wild Chesapeake oysters mingle in icy trays with farm-raised locals such as Hollywoods, Skinny Dippers or Chincoteagues. Blue Points are recruited from Connecticut to join in the festivities. Middleneck clams are welcome members of this briny bivalve team, and crowds of steamed shrimp, mussels, and snow crab legs cheer from the sidelines.

Baltimore

The bustling restaurant is a tribute to Chesapeake traditions in both the décor and cuisine. Vintage signs, watermen photos and crab pots on the wall pay homage to Bay heritage. Even the restroom doors are painted with old-fashioned pictures of animated oysters. The food is excellent, and the menu focuses on seafood caught nearby. You won't leave hungry after eating signature crab cakes, fried oyster platters, cast iron shrimp with grits, Natty Boh fish and chips, and bubbling New England steamer pots packed with ocean edibles. Beef tenderloin, Old Bay wings and grilled chicken sandwiches make meat lovers grin.

Nick's is located in Baltimore's industrial Locust Point where brick and steel warehouses provide a backdrop for boats cruising along the waterfront. The outdoor deck is a perfect place to sip an Orange Crush, listen to live music and enjoy a rosy sunset over Hanover Street Bridge. Built in 1916, the bridge's graceful arches are surrounded by four stone towers that meet in the middle to support a drawbridge that opens to accommodate boat traffic on the Patapsco River.

58 Northern Maryland

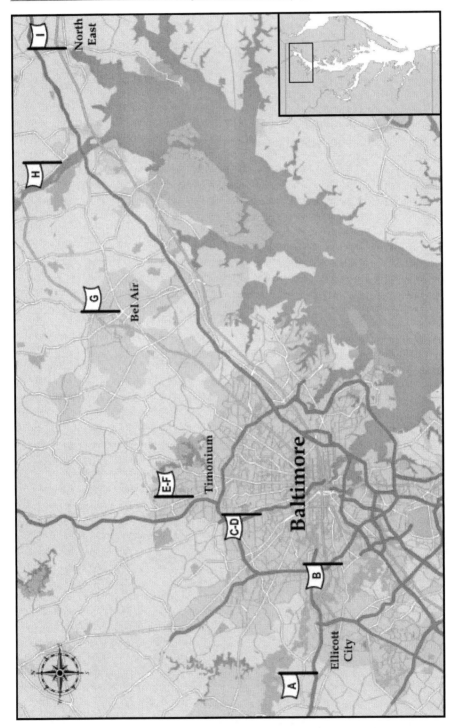

Northern Maryland

- Ⓐ Grille 620 60
- Ⓑ Catonsville Gourmet Market & Fine Foods 62
- Ⓒ The Mt. Washington Tavern 64
- Ⓓ The Nickel Taphouse.. 66
- Ⓔ Ryleigh's Oyster Hunt Valley 68
- Ⓕ Michael's Café Raw Bar & Grill 70
- Ⓖ Main Street Oyster House 72
- Ⓗ Lee's Landing Dock Bar 74
- Ⓘ Steak & Main 76

Northern Maryland

Grille 620

11099 Resort Road
Ellicott City, MD 21042
(410) 203-0620
www.grille620.com

Atmosphere Meter

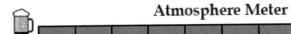

casual — formal

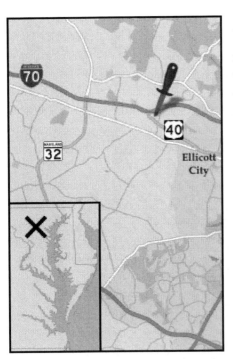

In the past, oyster bars belonged to the waterfront, in ports where boats pulled up to kitchen doors and unloaded their freshly tonged catch. But today's new wave of oyster houses is reaching beyond the city docks and into outlying suburbs where residential developments eagerly await their local bivalve deliveries.

Grill 620 is part of this growing trend of bringing oysters to inland towns all around the Chesapeake Bay watershed. And it's a welcome addition to a community anchored by Turf Valley Towne Square. Nestled into the new mall next to a stone fountain and fire pit, the restaurant's large white building is softened by red brickwork and an outdoor patio shaded with crimson umbrellas. It's a lovely setting with shoppers enjoying sunny days outdoors.

The spacious interior sports a contemporary yet comfortable décor, dividing the main room in half between the bar and dining areas. Beneath a high black ceiling stand pastel gray walls garnished with ornate mirrors and subtle artwork. Wood tables with candles generate a warm vibe.

Near the front door, shuckers place the standard cast of characters — oysters, clams, shrimp and lobster — on silver trays with ice and bundled lemons. During a recent visit, Chincoteagues (VA), Blue Points (CT) and Katama Bays (MA) took center stage on the oyster display.

The menu shows a strong affinity for seafood. Crab and artichoke dip and mussels steamed in white wine, tomatoes and garlic are among the favorites. Must-try entrees from the sea include crab cakes with Old Bay cole slaw, diver scallops with cauliflower puree and bouillabaisse with mussels, clams, shrimp, calamari and scallops in saffron anise broth. Steaks, beef sliders and roasted chicken are on tap for meat eaters.

Northern Maryland

Catonsville Gourmet Market & Fine Foods

829 Frederick Road
Catonsville, MD 21228
(410) 788-0005
www.catonsvillegourmet.com

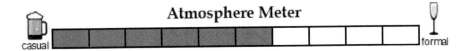

Atmosphere Meter

casual — formal

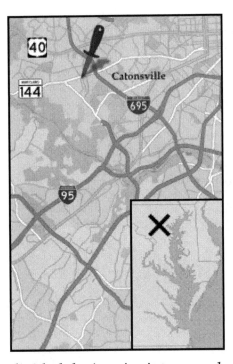

Urban oyster lovers who want a break from city life rave about visits to the Catonsville Gourmet Market. It's located on the main street of an idyllic getaway town. Streets are lined with lovely Victorian homes, old stone churches and long grassy lawns. Children scamper around playgrounds, and neighbors look up from tending their gardens to wave a welcoming hello.

In 2007, the restaurant moved into a quaint turn-of-the-century building and divided the interior into a market with gourmet take-out dishes and an attractive dining space with soothing gray walls, crisp white tablecloths, antique pictures and cherry wood furniture. They don't have a liquor license yet, but servers will gladly store your beer and wine in coolers and offer frosty mugs to keep beverages cold.

Oysters are a hot commodity here, with a guarantee of at least six different brands each week. During a recent visit, the list included Chincoteagues and Hog Islands from Virginia, Madhouses from Maryland, Blue Points from Connecticut, and Salt Ponds and Beavertails out of Rhode Island. The raw bar gets taken up a notch by adding sushi to the chilled selections of oysters, shrimp and mussels. A Chincoteague Roll tucks fried oysters, crab meat, sprouts and cucumber inside sticky rice and offers a red sauce for dipping.

Vintage wooden fish propped in the front window foreshadow a feast of fresh local seafood. Oysters Rockefeller, Old Bay steamed shrimp and prosciutto-wrapped scallops lead the appetizers, while lump crab cakes, fisherman's stew and pecan-crusted trout are highlights among the entrees. Beef, chicken and pork are also available.

The Mt. Washington Tavern

5700 Newbury Street
Baltimore, MD 21209
(410) 367-6903
www.mtwashingtontavern.com

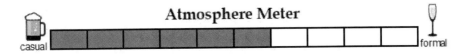

Atmosphere Meter

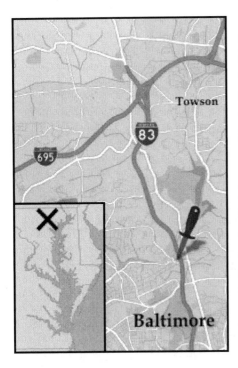

Mt. Washington Tavern's official address claims it's in Baltimore, but the pleasant wooded location along old train tracks feels more like a village outpost than a spot barely within the city limits.

The building, which locals say was an old market square, is big and takes up an entire block. A multi-alarm fire gutted the original structure in 2011, but thoughtful renovations and subtle Chesapeake décor have created a cozy place to meet for a bite and a brew.

The main floor is split into two sections. Dark wooden beams on the ceiling, stonework on the walls and brown leather booths give a muted tone to the first bar area. The second bar and dining room is flooded with light by vaulted ceilings, white walls and blonde wood floors. Vintage oyster cans and duck decoys rest on shelves above rows of windows. Fireplaces in both spaces take the edge off a winter eve, and the second floor deck embraces the warmth of summer.

The antique J.M. Clayton crab meat sign hanging above the bar underscores the restaurant's ties to the Bay, and the chalkboard above the shucker station announces the oysters of the week. Hollywoods from Maryland, Tavern Salts from Virginia, Salt Ponds from Rhode Island and Katama Bays out of Martha's Vineyard were featured during a recent visit.

J.O. spiced steamed shrimp and Maryland crab soup are ideal warm-up acts for tasty entrees such as oyster po' boys, rockfish and shrimp linguine, and fresh fish tacos. The Baltimore Club layers a seared crab cake with bacon, lettuce and tomato inside thick toasted white bread. Lamb burgers, steaks, sandwiches, chicken and pork are also on tap. Goat cheese potatoes au gratin and creamy mashed cauliflower are noteworthy side dishes.

Northern Maryland

The Nickel Taphouse

1604 Kelly Avenue
Baltimore, MD 21209
(443) 869-6240
www.nickeltaphouse.com

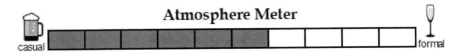

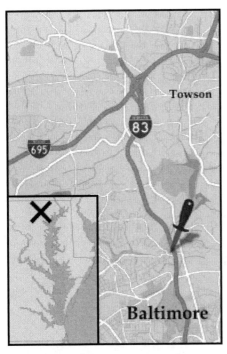

It's hard to take your eyes off the raw bar at Nickel Taphouse. The alluring display of oysters, ice and lemons is lit from above and imbedded into the wood bar. But the staff can break a bivalve aficionado's gaze by handing over the remarkable list of fresh oysters.

The inventory of 20 mollusks is categorized by brand, location and flavor description, with half pulled out of the Chesapeake Bay. Choptank Sweets, Skinny Dippers, Chesapeake Golds and Huckleberrys from Maryland compete for attention with Virginia's Broadwater Salts, White Stones, Battle Creeks, Olde Salts, Rappahannocks, and War Shores. Representatives from New York, Connecticut, Washington State and Canada add to the bastion of North American oyster flavors ranging from briny to creamy, mineral and pickle-like liveliness.

Just when it seems like life at Nickel Taphouse can't get any better, the waitress presents an equally impressive beer list with ales and lagers and stouts from New England to California. About 32 craft beers are on tap; the rest reside in bottles or cans. Many arrive from Maryland and Virginia to encourage local oyster parings that dare to cross state lines.

In addition to this plethora of oysters and brews, the menu is flush with innovative dishes filled with local fishes. Roasted oysters casino, Rockefeller, BBQ, curry and more hold their own against mussels steamed in Natty Boh and garlic. Cornmeal fried Chesapeake catfish, crab cakes and seared salmon swim to the table with cole slaw and duck fat potato chips. Burgers and chicken are also available.

After your order is sent to the kitchen, you can relax and enjoy the pleasing décor. Rich brown walls are adorned with vintage Bay photographs that give an old-fashioned saloon vibe. Exposed wooden beams and a chandelier made of deer antlers finish off a lively and pleasant atmosphere.

Northern Maryland

Ryleigh's Oyster Hunt Valley

22 West Padonia Road
Timonium, MD 21093
(410) 539-2093
www.ryleighs.com

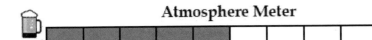

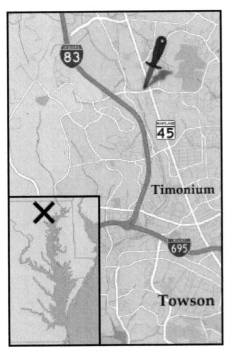

There's something mesmerizing about the entrance to Ryleigh's in Hunt Valley. The massive 15-foot oyster emblazed on the wall above a pristine white portico gives new meaning to the idea of "pearly gates." And if oysters could die and go to heaven, their paradise would surely look like this.

In contrast to its parent restaurant in a Federal Hill brownstone, the new Ryleigh's has taken a bland office complex and converted it into a vibrant sanctuary for oyster lovers where bivalves are honored in every corner. On the wood and brick walls hang understated nautical artwork, oyster tongs and dredges. Above a glass-encased shucker's station, delicate white lights twinkle inside a metal oyster cage. At two inside bars, servers pour oyster shooters, cocktails and craft beers to an energetic crowd.

Outdoors on the patio, drinks flow generously from the bar, musicians play on a small stage and families gather together to dine at wooden picnic tables and white Adirondack chairs. The atmosphere is upbeat, casual and welcoming.

Some people come for Oyster Hour, when $1 bivalves are accompanied by discounted drinks and dishes. Others convene to sample the weekly list of oysters that starts with Avery's Pearls, a plump sweet oyster grown at Hog Island, VA, exclusively for Ryleigh's. On a recent visit, the roll call included Skinny Dipper (MD), Shooting Point Salt (VA), Cotuit, Wellfleet and Wianno (MA), Malpeque (PEI), Tatamagouche (NS) and Umami (RI).

The menu reads like a tribute to Chesapeake cuisine: local oysters come char-grilled or fried, crab cakes are pan-sautéed Eastern Shore style, shrimp are doused with Old Bay, and littleneck clams arrive piping hot from the steamer. Wings, burgers, sandwiches and steaks round out the dining options.

Northern Maryland

Michael's Café Raw Bar & Grill

2119 York Road
Timonium, MD 21093
(410) 252-2022
www.michaelscafe.com

Atmosphere Meter

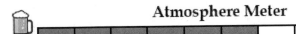

casual — formal

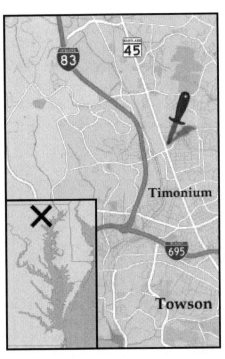

The wood and slate chalkboard hanging on the wall at Michael's Café is proof that they are serious about oysters. Nearly 30 brands make the list from New England, Mid-Atlantic, West Coast and Canadian aquafarms. Round stickers next to their names highlight which ones are available when you visit.

Chesapeake Bay oysters play a prominent role in the selections. Virginia varieties include Battle Creeks, War Shores, Chincoteagues, Rappahannocks and Olde Salts. Many of Maryland's favorites also make the grade — Choptank Sweets, Hollywoods, Chesapeake Golds and Barren Islands — to name a few.

Even though Michael's means business about bivalves, the Beat the Clock Happy Hour sets a light-hearted tone and creates a fun feeding frenzy with oysters. Here's how it works: at 3:00 p.m. oysters cost 75 cents, at 4:00 they go for $1, at 5:00 you pay $1.25, and at 6:00 they inch up to $1.50 each. The early bird catches the worm — or the bargain bivalve.

The restaurant is divided into two spaces with distinctly different atmospheres. One half feels like a neighborhood tavern with a large center bar commanding a good portion of the room. The other newer part has an open contemporary vibe with panels of windows and a sleek bar set against the wall. The outdoor patio, equipped with a full-service bar, gracefully combines wood and stone dividers with chrome tables and chairs to set a carefree mood.

The menu presents a delicious medley of seafood, steaks, sandwiches and specials. Fried oysters, colossal crab cakes, stuffed shrimp and crab imperial pay homage to the region's fresh catch. Chicken Chesapeake, crowned with creamy crab imperial, is a noble culinary pleasure on a platter.

Northern Maryland

Main Street Oyster House

119 South Main Street
Bel Air, MD 21014
(443) 371-7993
www.osterbarbelair.com

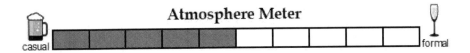

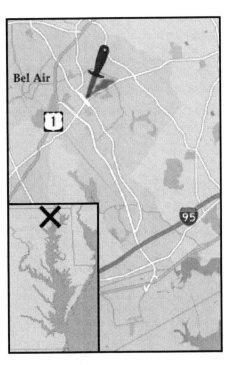

It's difficult to miss Main Street Oyster House when you drive into Bel Air. On the exterior wall of a building erected before the Civil War are gigantic murals that honor the men behind the scenes of Chesapeake seafood. On the left side of the painting is an oysterman in a black woolen cap trying to stave off the cold while leaning over a trough of mollusks. To the right, a crew of stoic watermen pulls in a bounty of oysters among relentless and frigid waves.

Inside is a restaurant worthy of such epic oyster artwork. Unfinished wood walls in the spacious downstairs dining rooms are decorated with vintage signs and pictures of fish and other aquatic creatures. New renovations brought the total number of bars to five. The main bar is made of wood with a marble top and is considered the longest bar in the county. Signature cocktails are exceptional. Bands play cover-free on weekends; the vibe is fun and electric.

In the center of it all is a shucking station with glass enclosures that reflect the smiling faces of people reading the chalkboard's list of oysters. Featured on a recent visit was a splendid assortment of Ropewalk Liberties, Harris Locals, Broadwaters and White Stones from Virginia; Skinny Dippers and Huckleberrys out of Maryland; Blue Points from New York; and Malpeques from Prince Edward Island.

Whether you dine indoors or upstairs on a rooftop deck, the kitchen staff and servers bend over backward to deliver an outstanding meal. Oysters kick off the appetizers: baked with garlic butter and parmesan cheese, topped with crab imperial or broiled Rockefeller style. Crispy oyster and shrimp po' boys come on toasted hoagie rolls with chipotle mayo. The Eastern Shore Steampot is a bubbling cauldron of seafood, corn and potatoes. Steaks, chicken and pork are also on tap.

Northern Maryland

Lee's Landing Dock Bar

600 Rowland Drive
Port Deposit, MD 21904
(443) 747-4006
www.leeslandingdockbar.com

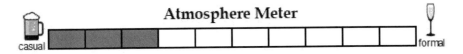

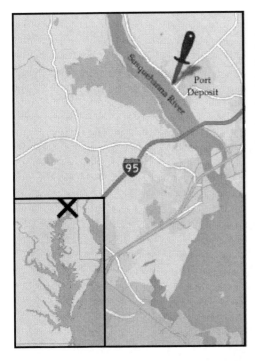

Now that aquafarmers have ended the myth of only consuming oysters in months with the letter "R" and made bivalves available year-round, you can add them to your list of summer pleasures. And the place to indulge in warm weather mollusk-eating is Lee's Landing Dock Bar.

It's located just off the main street in a gorgeous town with quaint homes, shops and taverns nestled into the rocky side of a hill. The waterfront view presents a conga line of bridges that span the Susquehanna River leading to the Chesapeake Bay. Palm trees encircle a massive 3,000-foot wooden deck, and a tiki bar at the water's edge serves cool blender drinks along with icy trays of oysters. Factor in a pirate ship playground for kids and 1,100 feet of free dockage for boaters, and everyone is ready to kick back and have a splendid time.

When new owners renovated the space in 2014, they created a laid-back venue for good food in a comfortable setting. Walls of knotty reclaimed wood are accented with colorful vintage signs for oysters, fishing lures and seafood. Above the raw bar station, an oversized shucking knife and oyster shell are tangled in a fisherman's net. The shucker opens a couple different brands of Chesapeake oysters every week, and Blue Points are regulars on the menu.

The kitchen staff devotes most of its attention to fresh local seafood. Oysters on the half shell, jumbo shrimp cocktail and crab claw martini lead the chilled choices. Steamer pots filled with middleneck clams or Prince Edward Island mussels come with French bread for dipping into the savory broth. Fried oyster po' boys, seared rockfish tacos and crab cakes present the best of the Bay. Burgers and chicken are available for landlubbers. (Note: Lee's Landing closes for a few months in the winter, so be sure to call ahead to make sure it's open.)

76 Northern Maryland

Steak & Main

107 South Main Street
North East, MD 21901
(410) 287-3512
www.steakandmain.com

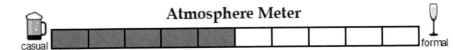

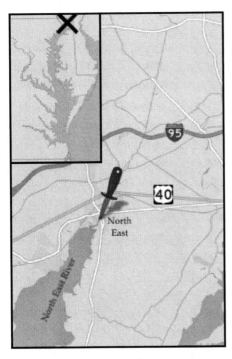

Chance encounters with mermaids during an oyster quest are considered a sign of good fortune. These mythical sea nymphs have impeccable taste in seafood and are known for revealing Neptune's hidden treasures to sailors and oyster seekers.

At Steak & Main, large vintage mermaid portraits hung above wooden booths send a signal that you found a slice of oyster heaven. In one picture, a mermaid toys with a treasure chest overflowing with pearls. Another painting depicts a water spirit looking sultry among the waves. And you might find mermaids printed on the antique oyster cans on shelves above the bar.

During the week, the oyster selection is limited to a few, but on weekends, bivalve choices rebound to offer a nice variety from the Chesapeake Bay and Mid-Atlantic regions. Chilled oysters with wasabi caviar are spicy and flavorful. Warm bivalve dishes include oyster stew, Rockefeller, crab imperial and quick-fried with panko bread crumbs.

Drunken Clams go on a binge with garlic, bacon bits and wine, and Big Bang Shrimp are fried to a perfect tempura puff and accompanied by Asian slaw. Burgers and sandwiches are hearty dishes, but the main attraction for carnivores is steak. A recent Travel Channel program honored the kitchen with the #1 steak in American restaurants, drawing Man Vs. Food's Tony Luke to the table to take the 5 ½-pound steak challenge.

With the exception of the celebrity's cameo appearance, this otherwise quiet town is a charming getaway destination. The restaurant, which is comprised of two conjoined Victorian buildings, accommodates both casual and dressy diners. The covered patio in front of the oyster bar creates an idyllic setting for bivalve eating and people watching.

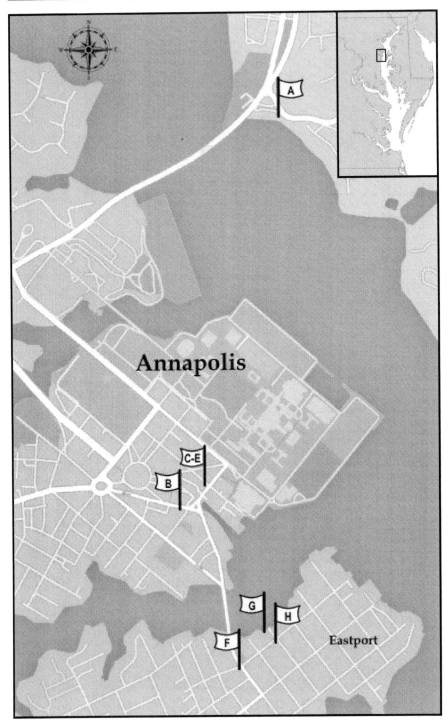

Annapolis & Eastport

- Ⓐ Severn Inn 80
- Ⓑ O'Brien's Oyster Bar & Steakhouse 82
- Ⓒ Yellowtail at the Market House 84
- Ⓓ McGarvey's Saloon & Oyster Bar 86
- Ⓔ Middleton Tavern 88
- Ⓕ Blackwall Hitch Annapolis 90
- Ⓖ Carrol's Creek Waterfront Restaurant 92
- Ⓗ Boatyard Bar & Grill 94

Annapolis & Eastport

Severn Inn

1993 Baltimore Annapolis Boulevard
Annapolis, MD 21409
(410) 349-4000
www.severninn.com

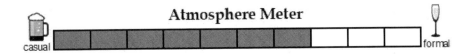

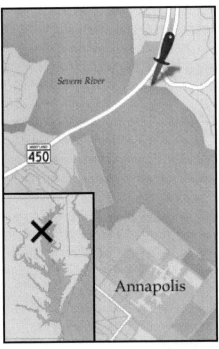

Severn Inn is more than just a pretty location. With waterfront decks offering a panoramic view of the river, historic Annapolis and U.S. Naval Academy, it could rest on its laurels and attract guests with lovely nautical eye candy.

The inside is quite swanky, too. White cloths are draped over light wood tables, and black-and-white photographs of Chesapeake watermen and boats hang on pale gray walls.

However, the main focal point for bivalve enthusiasts are the vintage oyster cans ceremoniously placed over the long mahogany bar. The impressive collection serves as a tribute to the world's infatuation with Bay oysters that reached a heyday in the 19th century and are making a comeback today.

The menu echoes the can compilation's affection for Chesapeake oysters with samplings of bivalves from the Bay's unique waterways. Tom's Coves from Chincoteague, VA, offer a briny Southern experience, while Barren Islands from Hoopers Island, MD, present the sweet buttery flavors of the northern region. Blue Points (CT) and Malpeques (PEI) are also in attendance. Wild Chesapeake Oysters come with tomato bacon jam and grilled bread.

As a self-proclaimed modern American seafood house, Severn Inn takes Chesapeake classics and dresses up the dishes with new fresh flavors. Maryland crab cakes saunter to the table with broccolini and corn salad, pan-seared rockfish is accompanied by roasted squash salsa, and seafood cobb salad arranges shrimp and crab on a bed of iceberg lettuce with bacon and hard-boiled egg. You can select dishes from a casual pub menu or from the elevated dinner menu that changes with the season. Either way, you're certain to enjoy a pleasant dining experience along the water.

Annapolis & Eastport

O'Brien's Oyster Bar & Steakhouse

113 Main Street
Annapolis, MD 21401
(410) 268-6288
www.obriensoysterbar.com

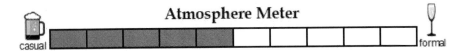

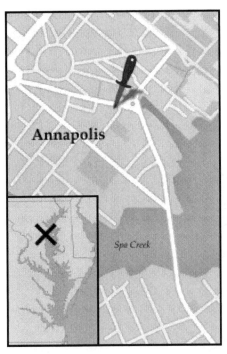

If the walls at O'Brien's Oyster Bar could talk, they'd have wondrous tales to tell about Annapolis and the characters who have floated into town. Built in 1774 as the Rose & Crown, the tavern was a favorite watering hole for Red Coats and rebellious colonists alike.

During the 1800s, when oysters were at their peak in the Bay, the place became a meeting house and dance hall. After World War II, it served Annapolis's first pizza, and during the 1970s, it was named after owner Fran O' Brien who played as a defensive lineman for the Washington Redskins. Some people believe that a ghost resides inside, but most patrons say the only spirits here come from the bartender.

Chesapeake Oyster Lovers' Handbook

Annapolis & Eastport

The décor combines the themes of a sports bar and historic landmark under one roof. Artwork fluctuates between photos of local sports heroes and old Clipper ships. The front room leans toward modern, with flat-screen TVs showing a menagerie of athletic events. The back dining room has a more sedate atmosphere, with a long salad bar and glass sneeze guard that harkens back to that '70s Redskins era. It's a busy place, frequented by locals, tourists, state government staffers and Navy midshipmen.

Local seafood and steaks are timeless features on the menu. Oysters are shucked at the raw bar near the front. Choices vary weekly, but regulars include Choptanks, Blue Points and bivalves from Chesapeake and Delaware bays. Chilled oysters, clams, shrimp, mussels and snow crab legs are laid out on ice. Oysters Rockefeller and clams casino show the rewards of running bivalves under a broiler. The rest of the menu offers enough meat and seafood options to make everyone, including the ghost, happy to be at O'Brien's.

Annapolis & Eastport

Yellowtail at the Market House

25 Market Space
Annapolis, MD 21401
(443) 852-2300
www.markethousedeli.com

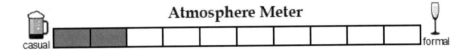

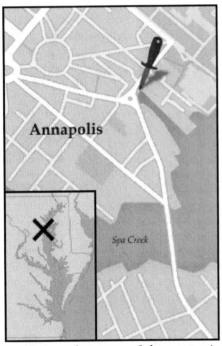

The Market House at the tip of Annapolis city dock sat vacant for quite some time, until Land & Sea Group Inc. revived the central location with vendors selling all kinds of wares from corned beef sandwiches to cappuccino, pizza and oysters. The place bustles with pedestrians dashing in and out with an eclectic array of food.

Yellowtail is the seafood component of the town square offering fresh local catch in a fast casual format. Amidst the lively scene, one personal appears to be at a standstill — the oyster shucker. His back and legs seem frozen, but his hands deftly move shells from bucket to board. With a flick of the wrist and a twist of his knife, he clips the mollusks' adductor muscle to release the plump meat inside. Spectators smile with gratitude as he removes tiny flecks of shell and sand.

Glacial mounds of ice keep the oysters chilled until ready to serve. Most of them are locally grown in Maryland and Virginia, but Blue Points from Long Island Sound make it to the regular list. On a recent visit, the shucker offered a good price for two brands from the Eastern Shore: Hungars Creeks and Cape Charles Oysters. A pound of perfectly pink steamed shrimp with fries created a tasty seafood combo.

Yellowtail is a delightfully simple seafood market that sticks to the basics. Chalkboards give the market price of crab cakes, oysters, shrimp and shellfish, and upside-down metal buckets serve as lampshades. The atmosphere is boisterous, bright and welcoming.

Patio furniture and concrete benches outside provide front row seats for a glorious view of the boats cruising into the dock. It is a wonderful place to take a long lunch with a friend on a warm spring day.

Annapolis & Eastport

McGarvey's Saloon & Oyster Bar

8 Market Space
Annapolis, MD 21401
(410) 263-5700
www.mcgarveysannapolis.com

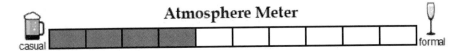

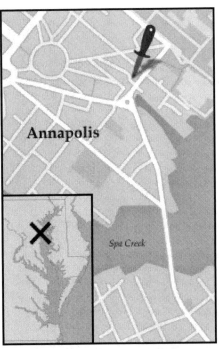

When you walk in the front entrance of McGarvey's turn-of-the-century saloon, you can easily imagine hardy sea captains, hard-working shipbuilders, and robust businessmen puffing on cigars and raising frothy mugs of beer.

Erected in 1871, the building's antique light fixtures, stained glass behind liquor bottles and nautical artwork on dark brick walls pay homage to the city's maritime traditions.

Down a few steps into the dining room, a slightly different vibe is set by the bar's owner. A former pilot and avid sailor, he brightened the space by placing a massive ficus tree in the center and lodging a large model airplane in its branches. Aviator helmets are lined up on a wooden shelf.

Annapolis & Eastport

While oyster enthusiasts admire the unique décor, their attention is quickly diverted when they notice a pair of dedicated shuckers at the back of the room. Their oyster station is filled with ice and surrounded by stools for watching bivalves get opened and placed on silver trays.

The raw bar showcases local oysters and clams harvested in Maryland, Virginia and Delaware. They are medium size and moderate salinity, and are delivered fresh six days a week, along with New England mussels and Texas Gulf Coast shrimp. The Waterman's Seafood Sampler steams them all together in an overflowing platter of bivalve bliss.

The regular menu follows a seafood motif with specialties from the Chesapeake region and beyond. Crab cakes are crafted with only a whisper of filler, and sea scallops are broiled with a fine coat of garlic-herb butter.

Clams casino and Oysters Rockefeller come from the kitchen piping hot and delicious. Shrimp are doused with Old Bay spice. Meat eaters won't feel neglected here. Aviator wings with fiery Buffalo sauce, char-grilled burgers and bratwurst with sauerkraut and melted Swiss guarantee a satisfied crowd.

Chesapeake Oyster Lovers' Handbook

Annapolis & Eastport

Middleton Tavern

2 Market Space
Annapolis, MD 21401
(410) 263-3323
www.middletontavern.com

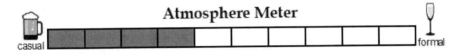

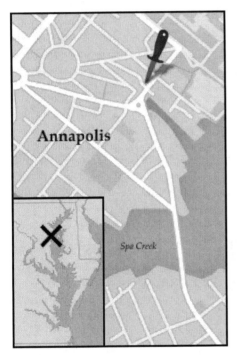

According to local lore, our founding fathers often visited Middleton Tavern. But did they dine on oysters? Most likely, yes. Built in 1750, the pub was a popular watering hole when colonial revolutionaries were stirring up trouble for the King. Oysters were so plentiful that they provided a good winter protein for every social class from slaves to merchants.

Because of his dental issues, George Washington liked to eat soft foods and seafood. Records show he often bought bushels of oysters for his family's table, and Martha's cookbook contained several oyster recipes. Thomas Jefferson, our first gourmet president, had an adventurous palate and his kitchen staff was trained in French cooking. He was so fond of oysters, crabs and shad that he kept charts of the seasons when they were sold at local markets.

Annapolis & Eastport **89**

If Middleton Tavern served as many oysters in the 1700s as it does today, then patrons have binged on bivalves at these tables for more than 250 years. Renovations in 1983 enhanced the space, added an oyster bar and retained a comfortable historic tavern atmosphere. Its covered front patio offers a fantastic view of the bustling Annapolis city dock.

Oyster shooters with Middleton Oyster Ale kick off the raw bar, followed by local bivalves such as Choptank Sweets and Chesapeake Golds. Mussels, clams and shrimp are steamed to order, and Oysters Rockefeller are topped with the traditional spinach and hollandaise. Steam pots bubble with snow crab legs, shrimp, potatoes, andouille sausage and corn. Local catch is a high priority with dishes such as crab cakes, pan-seared rockfish and crab-stuffed flounder. The menu also appeals to meat eaters by offering steaks, chicken, prime rib and veal parmesan. Pasta, soup, sandwiches and salads provide lighter fare options.

Annapolis & Eastport

Blackwall Hitch Annapolis

400 Sixth Street
Annapolis, MD 21403
(410) 263-3454
www.theblackwallhitch.com

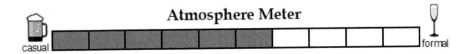

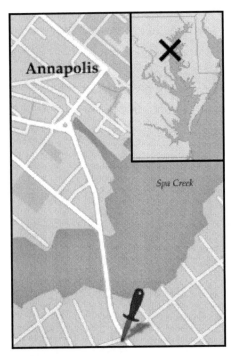

Since its doors opened in 2014, Blackwall Hitch Annapolis has extended a hearty welcome to oyster admirers. The lovely marble-top oyster bar, which spans the entire back of the dining room, reserves a special spot to discuss the growing list of Chesapeake oysters and the rise in regional aquaculture.

Written on the black chalkboard during a recent visit were Barren Islands (MD), Blue Points (CT), Chincoteagues (VA) and Patty's Fatty's (a hometown favorite). The selection of innovative oyster shooters and plates challenges bivalve buddies to explore new flavor sensations. The Fig Oyster Rita shooter glows with tequila, lime juice and pureed figs, and Dublin Donkey dunks an oyster in ginger beer, Irish whiskey and lime juice. Creative bivalve platters follow suit with standouts such as Hot Thai (roasted with wakame seaweed salad and rooster sauce), Curry (served with coconut milk, curry, slaw and toasted coconut) and Annapolitan (topped with a petite crab cake).

The menu is flush with fresh seafood that's prepared well in regional ingredients. Starters include sautéed shrimp with white wine and Creole butter, steamed PEI mussels with warm artisan bread, and seared ahi tuna. Entrees range from classic crab cakes and Chesapeake seafood steamers to Eastern Shore chicken pot pies and braised short ribs.

The décor is bright, contemporary nautical and quite beautiful, and an upstairs deck invites the sunshine to join your meal. After an exceptional dining experience, some diners wonder why the name sounds more like a law firm than a restaurant. In the 1800s, London's Blackwall Port was a launch pad for immigrants heading to the Bay area. Docking ships was difficult in the turbulent Chesapeake waters, so mates devised the "Blackwall hitch knot" to draw ropes tighter as vessels rose and fell with the tides.

Annapolis & Eastport

Carrol's Creek Waterfront Restaurant

410 Severn Avenue
Annapolis, MD 21403
(410) 263-8102
www.carrolscreek.com

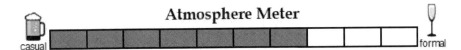

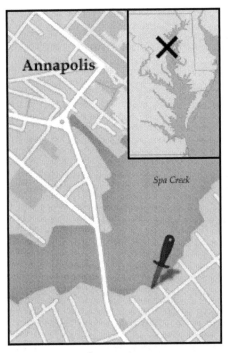

Charles Carroll was a Maryland patriot who risked his life by signing the Declaration of Independence. His mansion still stands on the other side of Spa Creek from where Carrol's Creek Restaurant proudly bares his name. (The different spellings come from a typo in a 1781 map.)

The drawbridge that connects the banks of the waterway is a sight best savored from the restaurant's outdoor decks. Leafs slowly open, asking cars to wait patiently while tall sailboats glide underneath, down the creek and into Annapolis marina. The restaurant's spectacular waterfront view extends beyond the drawbridge to reveal the capital dome, historic church steeples, other local landmarks and seafaring vessels. The stellar setting creates an exquisite location for eating oysters.

If uncooperative weather drives you indoors, you won't be disappointed. The spacious dining room's floor-to-ceiling windows conveniently bring the view to you. The lounge's contemporary décor is topped with neon blue stripes, and it's encircled by an extensive wine and spirits collection. Behind the bar is an ice chest display of seafood that will whet your appetite for a fine feast ahead.

Regional oysters pulled daily from Maryland and Virginia waters are served on the half shell. Harris Prides (MD) often top the list of favorites. Don't leave without trying Baked Oysters Carrol's Creek — the delicious house specialty topped with horseradish, bacon and cheddar cheese. You can choose between small sharing plates or full entrees of crab, shrimp, middleneck clams, mussels and tuna. Grilled steaks and sautéed chicken breasts are on hand for meat eaters.

Annapolis & Eastport

Boatyard Bar & Grill

400 Fourth Street
Annapolis, MD 21403
(410) 216-6206
www.boatyardbarandgrill.com

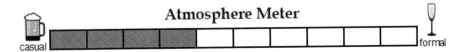

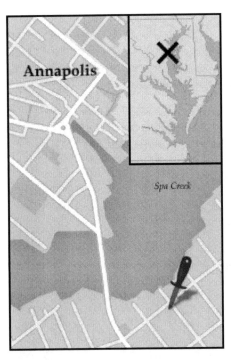

Most Bay communities have one special bar where locals like to go. It's the hot spot to hear the latest gossip, sell your boat or boast about the big fish you caught that day. Boatyard is Eastport's answer to a neighborhood pub — and it's a fine place for eating local oysters.

The owner, who grew up fishing and sailing on the Chesapeake, established the restaurant in 2001 as a home away from home for sailors, watermen, friends and families. It's part of the One Percent Club of businesses nationwide that donate a portion of their sales to environmental projects, and shells from the kitchen are recycled by Oyster Recovery Partnership.

The atmosphere is casual, energetic and festive. Walls are covered with a cacophony of mounted trophy fish, framed pictures of sailboats and nautical posters that celebrate Chesapeake life. Plastic skates and fish hang from the dining room ceiling, and the bar is shaped like a ship's hull with curved lines and a polished wood trim.

In the back stands the raw bar with signs above ice-filled cases announcing the daily selection of oysters, clams, mussels and shrimp. At least four Maryland and Virginia brands are usually listed, with Chincoteagues, Blue Points and Patty's Fatty's leading the pack of favorites.

Antoine's Stuffed Oysters, baked New Orleans style with spinach, shallots and cheese, are a scrumptious must-try dish. Same goes with the smoked fish of the day. Award-winning crab cakes are made with a hint of filler, and conch fritters are laced with Caribbean seasoning and served with traditional Bahamian sauce. To make sure everyone loves his meal, the extensive menu offers steaks, burgers, chicken, sandwiches, salads and pizzas — all served with warm Bay hospitality.

96 DC's Maryland Suburbs & Southern Maryland

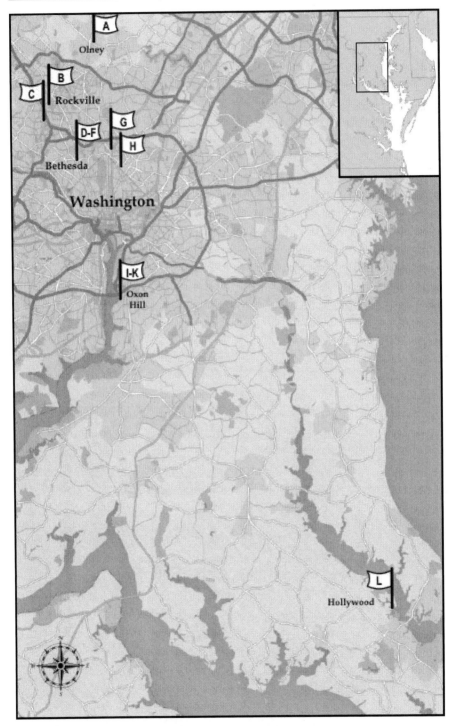

Chesapeake Oyster Lovers' Handbook

DC's Maryland Suburbs & Southern Maryland

DC's Maryland Suburbs & Southern Maryland

- Ⓐ GrillMarX Restaurant & Raw Bar 98
- Ⓑ Clyde's Tower Oaks Lodge 100
- Ⓒ The Grilled Oyster Company 102
- Ⓓ Black's Bar & Kitchen 104
- Ⓔ Mussel Bar & Grille Bethesda 106
- Ⓕ Food Wine & Co. 108
- Ⓖ All Set Restaurant & Bar 110
- Ⓗ Republic 112
- Ⓘ McLoone's Pier House National Harbor 114
- Ⓙ McCormick & Schmick's Harborside at National Harbor 116
- Ⓚ The Walrus Oyster & Ale House 118
- Ⓛ Stoney's Seafood House Clarke's Landing 120

Chesapeake Oyster Lovers' Handbook

98 DC's Maryland Suburbs & Southern Maryland

GrillMarX Restaurant & Raw Bar

18149 Town Center Drive
Olney, MD 20832
(301) 570-1111
www.gmxsteak.com

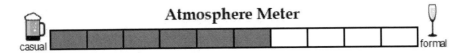

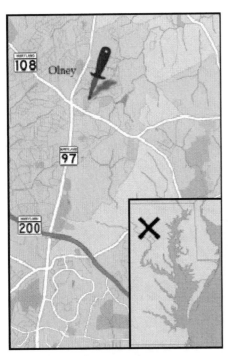

Like many oyster houses located in shopping malls, GrillMarX is proof that the emerging oyster craze is not just an urban phenomenon. Suburban bivalve fans who don't want to deal with city traffic or parking headaches are asking chefs to bring the oysters to them. And they will eat plenty of bivalves, especially when served next to a sizzling steak.

Tucked between an ice cream shop and a grocery store, this lovely restaurant is full of pleasant surprises and counters stereotypes of strip mall eateries. Right off the bat, guests are drawn to an outdoor patio with hanging flower baskets and powerful heaters to stave off cool weather.

The interior is much larger than it appears from the parking lot, and the sophisticated contemporary décor almost

DC's Maryland Suburbs & Southern Maryland

makes you feel like you're dining downtown. Exposed brick walls, plush burgundy fabric swags defining privacy areas, booths with cushioned leather seats and smooth wooden tables create a comfortable tavern feel. The bar area bustles with TVs showing sports and neighbors having fun.

At the front entrance in a glass-enclosed station, the shucker works diligently to keep up with customers' demands for oysters on the half shell. Blue Points and Malpeques are the regular standard bearers, but regional mollusks are occasionally folded into the mix, depending on the season. Littleneck clams and jumbo shrimp cocktail complete the chilled seafood selections. Cooks in the open kitchen crank out Maryland style crab cakes, grilled salmon and ahi tuna for fish lovers, but seared steaks and slow-roasted prime rib are the main attraction. Thick, juicy and flavorful, they are hard to resist. Salads, chicken, burgers and hearty sandwiches round out the menu options. (Note: GrillMarX recently opened another location in Clarksburg, MD.)

Clyde's Tower Oaks Lodge

2 Preserve Parkway
Rockville, MD 20852
(301) 294-0200
www.clydes.com/tower

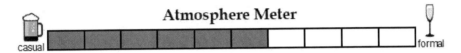

Atmosphere Meter

Washington, DC, locals who are accustomed to seeing Clyde's restaurants in city spots such as Chevy Chase, Chinatown and Georgetown will be astonished by the location in Rockville. Far away from the congested Rockville Pike, Tower Oaks Lodge is set in a wooded area next to a nature preserve.

It's a radical departure from the urban dining experience that began downtown in 1963. A brook flows through the trees near the front entrance, and the log and stone building looks like a camping lodge you'd discover during an Adirondack Mountains getaway. The centerpiece of this massive rural outpost is a 200-year old timber barn from Vermont with immense stone fireplaces at each end. The entire ceiling of one spacious room holds a giant twig sculpture that replicates

DC's Maryland Suburbs & Southern Maryland

the feeling of walking through a forest. One space is decorated with birch bark canoes, oars, duck decoys, antlers, stuffed critters, fishing lures and other artifacts; another room sports a horse hunt theme. An arched walkway with sparkly lights attached to sapling branches joins the sections.

It's big and boisterous and somehow blends oysters into the great outdoors motif. The shucker's list carries at least six brands each week, including Barnstables (MA), Harpswell Flats and Permaquids (ME), Navy Points (NY) and Salt Ponds (RI). Other raw bar merry men are shrimp and clams.

The extensive menu is swimming with seafood dishes such as shrimp linguine, Chesapeake Bay blue catfish, jumbo lump crab cakes and Clyde's irresistible cream of crab soup. Grilled oysters are topped with butter, basil and parmesan. Meat eaters rekindle the campfire experience when they cut into thick steaks, burgers, duck breast and roasted chicken.

Chesapeake Oyster Lovers' Handbook

102 DC's Maryland Suburbs & Southern Maryland

The Grilled Oyster Company

7943 Tuckerman Lane
Potomac, MD 20854
(301) 299-9888
www.thegrilledoystercompany.com

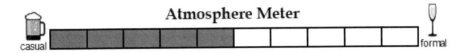

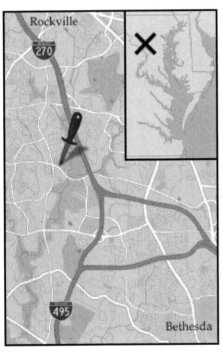

In Potomac's Cabin John Shopping Center, you can discover a hidden gem oyster sanctuary called The Grilled Oyster Company. Its unassuming exterior façade with a small outdoor patio almost disguises the big excitement for oysters that simmers inside.

At the front of the restaurant stands a bartender who is knowledgeable about regional bivalves. As he recites the daily oyster list without glancing once at the large chalkboard back in the dining room, you feel your belly start to rumble with eager anticipation of a Chesapeake bivalve feast.

The weekly oyster inventory contains a fine selection of brands, mostly from Maryland and Virginia. On a recent visit, local choices included Barren Islands, Chesapeakes and Wild

DC's Maryland Suburbs & Southern Maryland

Ass Ponies (MD), War Shores and Battle Creeks (VA), and Salt Ponds (RI). The variety sends taste buds on a seamless journey from buttery sweet to crisp and briny. As an added bonus in October, the restaurant runs $1 oyster specials on Tuesdays, and Mussel Mondays present discounted platters of steamed mollusks with fries. Grilled oysters are scrumptious.

The décor is understated, pleasant and inviting. White linens cover the dining room tables, and a huge bronze crab hangs on a white painted brick wall. Cushioned tall-back booths along the wall give an ideal vantage point to examine a large chalkboard with daily specials, craft beers and oysters. The menu is inspired by the Bay's unique Eastern Shore cuisine. Chesapeake Chowder heats up a bowl with oysters, rockfish, bacon, corn and potatoes. Plump Maryland crab cakes come with spicy cole slaw, while seared rockfish arrives with brussel sprouts. Eastern Shore duck tacos and fried oyster po' boys achieve the right level of crunch.

DC's Maryland Suburbs & Southern Maryland

Black's Bar & Kitchen

7750 Woodmont Avenue
Bethesda, MD 20814
(301) 652-5525
www.blacksbarandkitchen.com

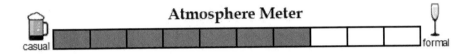

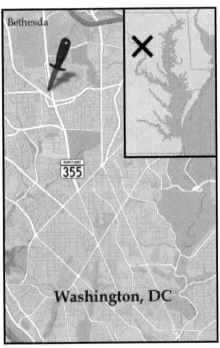

You could spend more than a year at Black's Bar trying every single pairing of oysters with wines, craft beers and specialty cocktails. Such a noble pursuit would lead you to a state-of-the-art temperature-controlled wine room with 300+ labels. Beer tastings would include local breweries such as Jailbreak and Denizens. Martini Time specials would introduce lovable libations like Lemon Drop, White Cosmo and Apple Martini.

Then you'd need to match brands or create a super-sampler from an impressive selection of boutique and premium oysters harvested in the Chesapeake waters and beyond. The most-wanted list during a recent visit was comprised of Old Black Salts (the house special), Sewansecotts and Battle Creeks (VA), Barren Islands

DC's Maryland Suburbs & Southern Maryland

(MD), Washburns (MA) and Ninigret Cups (RI). It's a big bivalve challenge that is sure to reap epicurean rewards.

Black's is a beautiful restaurant with a sleek modern design that's very easy on the eye. The outdoor patio is flanked by shade trees, and a stone pond mutes the city sounds. Two-story windows allow sunlight to enter and brighten the blonde wood walls. The vibe is energetic.

Chrome and ice dividers cut deep into the wooden bar signal an affinity for fresh regional seafood. Oysters, clams and shrimp top the chilled choices. Mussels are prepared three ways: Addie's (tomato and garlic), Thai (lemongrass, ginger and basil) and Malt Mussels (applewood smoked bacon, honey and mustard). Crisp cornmeal fried oysters are best dipped in a Creole tartar sauce. Must-try fish dishes: saffron-tomato seafood stew and sesame-crusted yellowfin tuna. Steak, duck and pork round out meat eaters' options.

106 DC's Maryland Suburbs & Southern Maryland

Mussel Bar & Grille Bethesda

7262 Woodmont Avenue
Bethesda, MD 20814
(301) 215-7817
www.musselbar.com

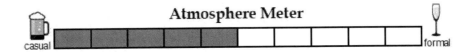

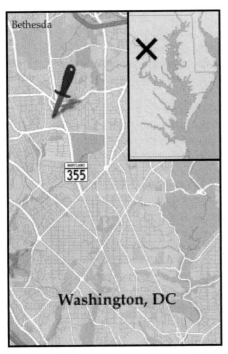

The French are renowned for their love of bivalves, but when Mussel Bar opened in July 2010, Bethesda was introduced to another European spin on mollusk mania.

This Belgian gastro pub shows that tiny countries can infuse gigantic flavors into bivalve dishes. The kitchen staff prepares mussels six different ways: white wine with roasted garlic, spicy Thai curry in coconut milk, mushroom and bacon in truffle cream, Mediterranean sausage and goat cheese in tomato broth, Bolognese with capers and shaved egg, and Provençal with tomatoes, garlic and basil. Each style is so uniquely delicious that you plan which flavor to try on your next visit. The presentation builds excitement about your meal. Mussels arrive piping hot in the pan and covered with a lid. When the top is popped, you

DC's Maryland Suburbs & Southern Maryland

receive a warm steam facial of savory herbs and spices. Thick artisan bread helps scoop up every drop of sauce, and the addictive French fries come with special mayos and ketchup.

It's an ideal place to double down on bivalves and eat an entire meal of mollusks. Penn Cove Mussels are shipped from Washington State, but most of the oysters are harvested in Maryland, Virginia and New England. Other seafood dishes include jumbo lump crab cakes, pan seared shrimp and scallops, and grilled salmon fillet. Onion soup topped with gruyere cheese should be required eating on wintry days.

This cozy restaurant would not be authentic Belgian if it didn't serve good beer. The list of brews here is staggering: 14 on tap, 156 in bottles and 24 in cans. You can take an international tour of ales from Belgium to Brooklyn and scores of foreign lands in between to find the perfect pairings that match your icy tray of local oysters.

108 DC's Maryland Suburbs & Southern Maryland

Food Wine & Co.

7272 Wisconsin Avenue
Bethesda, MD 20814
(301) 652-8008
www.foodwineandco.com

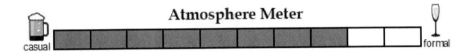

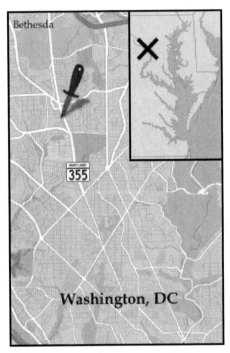

Fighting traffic on busy Wisconsin Avenue might make you overlook Food Wine & Co. Its dimly-lit burgundy awnings offer only a subtle announcement that a lovely upscale bistro waits inside. It's the kind of spot to keep in your back pocket for a good bite to eat after catching a movie at the theaters next door.

New owners took over a former pizza place and converted it into a charming restaurant with modern décor, subtle lighting and rich dark wood on the walls. A long bar is lined with cushy stools, and a massive clock hangs above the liquor bottles, creating a pleasant retreat for happy hour drinks. House specialty cocktails wash away the workday stress with smooth gin-based concoctions such as The Naturalist and Ginger Breeze. A second dining area is decorated with rows

Chesapeake Oyster Lovers' Handbook

of wine bottles stocked on tall shelves. The outdoor patio facing an interior courtyard feels like a secret hideaway.

The shucking station, with oysters prominently displayed on beds of ice, is the centerpiece of the main dining room. Sitting on barstools with your elbows on the creamy marble top and watching the shucker's slight of hand is half the fun. Depending on the season, you can sample three or four different brands of bivalves, mostly from Chesapeake Bay and East Coast aquafarms. Chincoteague, Olde Salt, Hollywood, Sweet Jesus, Montauk Point and Malpeque are members of this oyster bar's frequent flyers' club.

Fish ceviche, tuna tartare and diver scallop crudo join the raw bar roster, and the main menu features other seafood dishes such as fried calamari, charred octopus, cast-iron mussels and pan-roasted rockfish. Steaks, lamb, pork loin, chicken and vegetarian plates are also on tap.

All Set Restaurant & Bar

8630 Fenton Street
Silver Spring, MD 20910
(301) 495-8800
www.allsetrestaurant.com

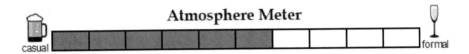

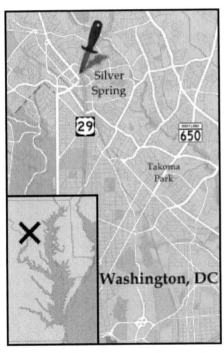

Silver Spring was once a fine-dining wasteland. It had a handful of places where you could get a decent meal, but if you wanted something new or special, you had to scoot across East-West Highway and forage around Bethesda. Fortunately, years of revitalization have started to attract adventurous chefs and exciting new restaurants to the budding downtown.

All Set is the seafaring newcomer positioned just off the main drag. It's located on the ground level of an office building, and its patio is landscaped with young maple trees and sea grass. A captain's compass on the sign sets the stage for nouveau-nautical décor inside. Bright navy blue seats reflect the color of the ocean waves, and screens made of knotted nautical rope serve as room dividers. Chandeliers made of capiz shells dangle from the rafters. It's bright and roomy, and upbeat music lifts the atmosphere.

With roots in New England fare, the chef puts a contemporary twist on coastal cuisine, appointing oysters and clams as his first mates. The list changes daily, but usually four Chesapeake and Atlantic brands are available. During a recent visit, a shiny chrome ice bin held signs brandishing oyster names such as Chincoteagues (VA), Holy Grails (MD), Malpeques (PEI) and Nasketuckets (RI). Happy Hour specials offer them for $1 each from 3:00 to 6:00 p.m. Littleneck clams, tuna tartare and cocktails of shrimp, crab or lobster are among the other raw bar treats.

Seafood dishes float throughout the menu featuring regional favorites: lobster rolls, clam chowder, crab cakes, steamed mussels and fish and chips. Chicken and beef are on tap, and sandwiches come with Cape Cod chips.

DC's Maryland Suburbs & Southern Maryland

Republic

6939 Laurel Avenue
Takoma Park, MD 20912
(301) 270-3000
www.republictakoma.com

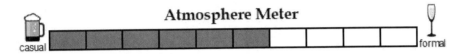

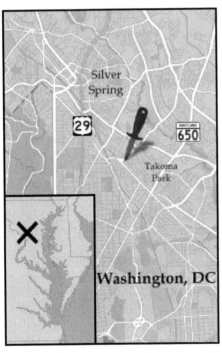

Republic is the latest member of Black Restaurant Group, which includes other oyster strongholds such as Pearl Dive and BlackSalt. And it's a welcome addition to the charming streets of Takoma Park.

The décor artfully blends the ambience of a bistro with a bordello and neighborhood pub, generating a unique vibe that makes you want to return as often as possible. Crimson crushed velvet seating rests against the wall under vintage wallpaper in the main dining room. Three arches of cherry wood frame the liquor shelves at the bar, and some of the seats are backed with faux zebra pelts. Strings of cheerful white lights crisscross above the patio out back, encouraging guests to kick back and relax. Live bands play on weekends, further enhancing the excellent groove.

As if this fantastic setting wasn't enough, Republic also scores big points with oyster explorers. Well known for its solid sampling from the Chesapeake, it also features bivalves grown on the Atlantic and West Coasts. During recent trips, Ugly Oyster and Barren Island (MD), Washburn, Battle Creek and Old Black Salt (VA), and Skookum and Goose Point (WA) were among the premium brands. Wood-grilled oysters and steamed mussels are heavenly.

The menu focuses on organically grown and seasonal ingredients. Seafood standouts include pan-seared Rhode Island skate wing and grilled Virginia catfish in coconut lime sauce. Vegetarians relish a daily special custom-made for their dietary needs. Carnivores enjoy plenty of choices, including slow-braised Pennsylvania pork belly, hanger steak with smoked bacon and fried farm egg, and Smith Meadows burgers with aioli on a toasted pretzel bun.

114 DC's Maryland Suburbs & Southern Maryland

McLoone's Pier House National Harbor

141 National Plaza
Oxon Hill, MD 20745
(301) 839-0815
www.mcloonespierhousenh.com

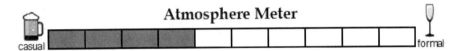

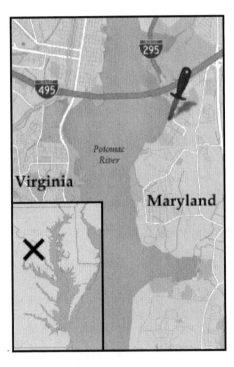

At McLoone's, every sunset deserves a celebration. That's why they hung a large digital clock at the bar to count the minutes until the sun goes down.

The other important time of day here is Happy Hour, when the price of oysters gets knocked down to $1.50 each. Bargain-hunting bivalve fans can choose from two or three different brands. Blue Points always make the list, along with a rotating selection from across the Chesapeake region.

Oysters Rockefeller and crispy fried oysters lead the bivalve charge on the menu, followed by pan-seared scallops with risotto and mussels steamed in white wine, tomatoes and shallots. The kitchen gives high priority to other types of local

DC's Maryland Suburbs & Southern Maryland 115

seafood. Standouts include Jamaican jerk red snapper served with coconut rice and peas, lump crab cakes with sweet potato puree and spinach, and jumbo stuffed shrimp in a lemon beurre blanc sauce. Chicken, beef, pork chops and ribs accommodate meat eaters.

    This location marks the first out-of-state restaurant for the New Jersey franchise, and the casual atmosphere fits well at National Harbor. Bold blue colors on the walls, umbrellas and even the wine glasses match the waves on the Potomac. Models of wooden sailboats, flags on the ceiling and nautical artwork prove they're ready to be part of the Bay. A row of fish tank windows that looks like portholes underscores the seafaring theme. Outside guests lounge on the expansive deck and take in a spectacular waterfront view of the Capital Wheel, Woodrow Wilson Bridge, Potomac River, Old Town Alexandria and convoys of boats pulling into the marina. The vibe is lively and fun.

Chesapeake Oyster Lovers' Handbook

McCormick & Schmick's Harborside at National Harbor

145 National Plaza
Oxon Hill, MD 20745
(301) 567-6224
www.mccormickandschmicks.com

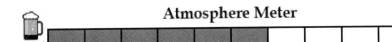

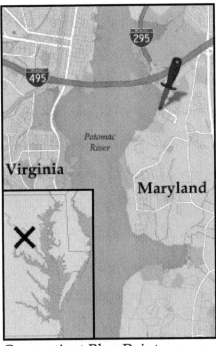

McCormick & Schmick's at National Harbor stands next to "The Awakening," a massive five-piece cast iron sculpture of a bearded giant breaking free from the earth. His huge outstretched hand looks like he's trying to reach into the restaurant and grab a big plate of Bay oysters.

He would be pleased by the varieties doled out by the shuckers. Skinny Dippers from Maryland, Stingrays and Chincoteagues harvested in Virginia, and Connecticut Blue Points are on the regular menu, with other local brands served occasionally, depending on the season. Jumbo shrimp cocktail, lump crab tower and tuna tartare come to the table chilled and fresh, while mussels arrive steaming hot with wine and herbs.

DC's Maryland Suburbs & Southern Maryland

The menu is split between creatures that swim in the ocean or graze on the land. Seafood specialties include Chesapeake Bay rockfish, Maryland crab cakes, stuffed Atlantic salmon and live Maine lobster. Cashew crusted tilapia with Jamaican rum butter is simply delicious. Steaks are the signature dish, but carnivores can also satisfy their whims with parmesan crusted chicken, Kobe beef burgers or tender beef medallions with roasted potatoes.

When M&S stretched out its iconic green awnings at the harbor in 2010, it scored a prime location in the hub of the waterfront activities, and the large wraparound patio offers an ideal vantage point for watching all the marina happenings. Inside the restaurant, the atmosphere is comfortable and not too formal. Rooms are decorated with a mixed theme of American politics and nautical life. The bar displays photos of former U.S. presidents and vintage campaign posters, and the dining areas are adorned with trophy fish and crab pictures.

DC's Maryland Suburbs & Southern Maryland

The Walrus Oyster & Ale House

140 Waterfront Street
Oxon Hill, MD 20745
(301) 567-6100
www.walrusoysterandale.com

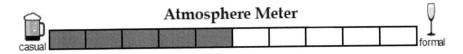

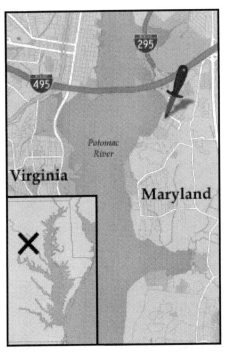

"The Walrus and the Carpenter" is a Lewis Carroll poem about four plump oysters that take a stroll on the beach and get eaten as a snack along with bread slathered with butter. A line from the tale is inscribed on the wall and serves as inspiration for The Walrus Oyster & Ale House.

When you come to this lovely place on a hill above the harbor, feel free to follow in the walrus's footsteps and devour as many bivalves as you please. A remarkable number of them are waiting in an icy display at the bar from local and East Coast aquafarms, namely Barren Island, Sweet Jesus and Chesapeake Gold (MD), Rappahannock, Chincoteague Salt, Barcat, Stingray, and James River (VA); Blue Point (NY), Wellfleet (MA) and Raspberry Point (PEI).

Other chilled delicacies include lobster, shrimp and Dungeness crab clusters. Seafood drives the menu with bivalve treats such as steamed mussels, middleneck clams, oysters Rockefeller, clams casino and pan-seared scallops. Deviled eggs are topped with fried MeTompkin oysters, hot cherry peppers and garlic aioli, fish and chips comes with hand-cut fries, and the lobster roll is served in thick buttered bread — just like in the poem! Craft beers help wash down every delicious bite. Meat eaters have a few options: blackened chicken and char-grilled rib eye steaks.

The space is open and contemporary, and the atmosphere is energetic. Wood and chrome furniture fills the room, and sunlight pours in through tall windows. Interesting artwork hangs near the back. A huge map of the Chesapeake Bay points out where the oysters on your plate are harvested, and a detailed timeline shows the history of local oysters from the 1800s to present day. Be sure to check them out.

DC's Maryland Suburbs & Southern Maryland

Stoney's Seafood House
Clarke's Landing

24580 Clarke's Landing Lane
Hollywood, MD 20636
(301) 373-3986
www.stoneysseafoodhouse.com/clarkeslanding

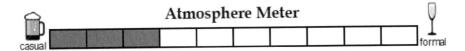

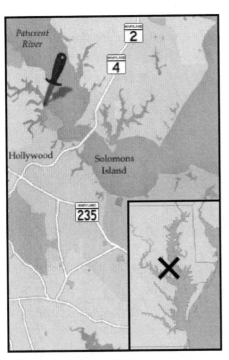

Stoney's Restaurant Group took the helm of this lovely waterfront location in 2014, and breathed new life into a beloved neighborhood pub. It's the kind of place where you experience easy Southern Maryland living firsthand and enjoy unique regional cuisine. The view of Gov. Thomas Johnson Bridge spanning the gentle waves of the Patuxent River is spectacular.

Guests are encouraged to kick back on the outdoor deck with a chilled beverage under the shade of blue beach umbrellas. Recent renovations give the interior dining rooms an updated and open look, yet vintage photographs of oyster shuckers and watermen

DC's Maryland Suburbs & Southern Maryland

underscore the restaurant's connection to Chesapeake heritage. The atmosphere is warm and welcoming.

In this laid-back picturesque setting, you can sample a nice collection of local and East Coast oysters. Blue Points, Chincoteagues and Island Creeks are featured on the regular menu. Boutique bivalves grown in nearby coves appear each week. Steamed or raw, these local oysters carry such a clean buttery flavor profile that ordering a dozen doesn't ever feel like enough. Shrimp, cherrystone clams, crab legs and mussels are testaments to freshness at the raw bar. Oysters Rockefeller are topped with spinach, mozzarella and bacon bits, and oysters imperial are crowned with crab meat.

Seafood rules in this house with flagship items such as crab cakes, blackened rockfish gyro (feta cheese and cucumber sauce in a warm pita pocket) and Korsnick's Kabobs (shrimp, scallops and veggies grilled on a stick). Burgers, steaks and BBQ chicken offer tasty options to meat eaters.

122 The Eastern Shore

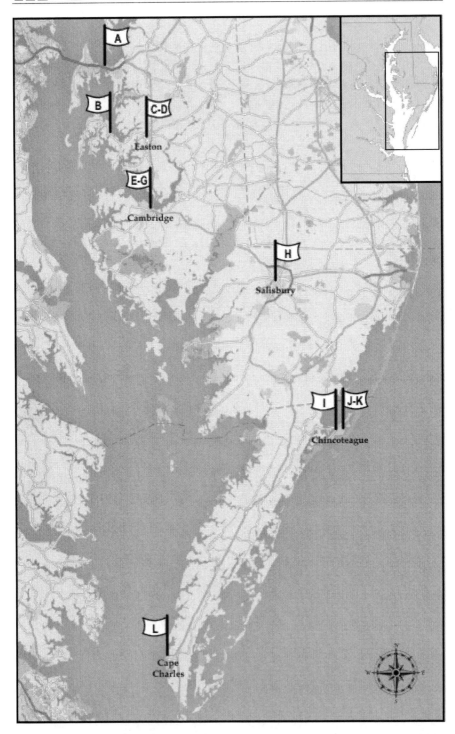

The Eastern Shore

- Ⓐ Harris Crab House 124
- Ⓑ Awful Arthur's Seafood Company 126
- Ⓒ Brasserie Brightwell 128
- Ⓓ Washington Street Pub & Oyster Bar 130
- Ⓔ Jimmie & Sook's Raw Bar & Grill 132
- Ⓕ Ocean Odyssey Restaurant 134
- Ⓖ Blue Point Provision Company 136
- Ⓗ Brew River Restaurant 138
- Ⓘ The Jackspot 140
- Ⓙ AJ's on the Creek 142
- Ⓚ The Village Restaurant 144
- Ⓛ Oyster Farm Seafood Eatery at Kings Creek 146

The Eastern Shore

Harris Crab House

433 Kent Narrow Way North
Grasonville, MD 21638
(410) 827-9500
www.harriscrabhouse.com

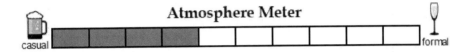

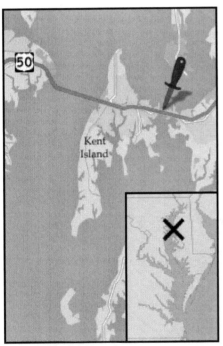

Imagine standing at an oyster buffet table — a bountiful self-serve station filled with a cornucopia of the Chesapeake's finest bivalves. Some are freshly shucked and carefully placed upon ice so not a single drop of their briny liquid is lost. Others wait in misty chafing dishes after being fried, steamed or baked Casino-style with a dusting of mild cheese. It's just you, a pair of tongs and all the oysters your heart desires.

This epicurean paradise runs from the first week of October until the end of April, but Harris gives plenty of other reasons to visit year-round. Since 1947, this three-generation family-owned seafood house has managed to uphold Chesapeake traditions while others fell by the wayside. Watermen arrive by boat or pickup truck to deliver their daily catch, harvested wild or grown at regional aquafarms on the shores of Maryland and the Delaware Bay. Everything here is fresh, from the creamy oyster stew to the Louisiana-style oyster po' boys on a toasted baguette.

Popcorn shrimp, grilled rockfish, stuffed flounder, steamed mussels or Cherrystone clams, and the classic all-you-can-eat Maryland crabs with Old Bay cover wooden tables in this classic waterside restaurant. Window seats present stellar views of sunsets over Kent Narrows Bridge. The walls are adorned with antique oyster cans and vintage posters of dancing bivalves and crabs.

To top it off, next door is Harris Seafood Company, one of the last oyster shucking houses left on the Bay. Inside workers line up at tables with knives in hand opening shells and tipping oysters into containers for shipment to local markets. You can buy oysters by the bag or already shucked in pint jars, and you can look inside the processing plant to witness a timeless slice of Chesapeake heritage.

Awful Arthur's Seafood Company

402 South Talbot Street
St. Michaels, MD 21663
(410) 745-3474
www.awfularthurs.com

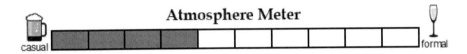

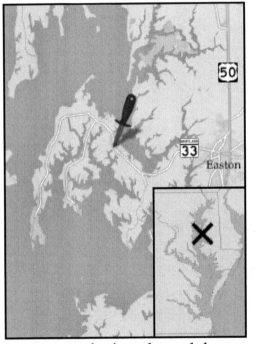

A lovely Victorian house stands on the main street of historic St. Michaels. Its gingerbread trim and wide front porch hearken back to a time when wild oyster reefs covered the shores of the Chesapeake. What makes this house different than other turn-of-the-century buildings in town? Something very modern is happening inside.

It's home to Awful Arthur's Seafood, a restaurant that's embraced the new wave of producing bivalves called aquaculture. Instead of dredging the Bay's bottom to hunt for oysters, today's aquafarmers are growing them in cages along the banks. The result is a burgeoning oyster population that's sustainable and available year-round. An aquaculture cage filled with oyster shells hangs on the wall near an outdoor patio, inviting guests to sample the bounty of boutique bivalves. They are listed on a card with brand names and descriptions of each oysters' flavor. On a recent visit, the roster touted Chesapeake Gold, Barren Island, Sewansecott, Chincoteague Salt, HongaTonk, Rappahannock, Olde Salt, Blue Point and James River.

Other oyster bar attractions include steamed middleneck clams, crawfish, mussels, spiced shrimp and snow crab legs. The chef adds a little heat to create delectable dishes such as oysters Rockefeller, oyster stew and po' boys. Seafood dominates the menu with jumbo lump crab cakes, blackened ahi tuna tacos and the unique lobster Ruebens. Burgers, chicken and hot dogs lure meat eaters to the table.

If the restaurant name sounds familiar, it's because you might have seen its Virginia operations in Richmond, Roanoke or Salem. This is the first location to enter Maryland, and everyone on the Eastern Shore is awfully glad that Awful Arthur's has come to town.

128 The Eastern Shore

Brasserie Brightwell

206 North Washington Street
Easton, MD 21601
(410) 819-3838
www.brasseriebrightwell.com

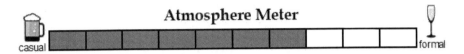

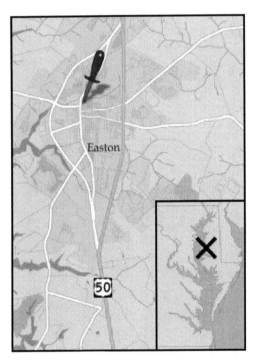

When the French poet Leon-Paul Fargue compared the taste of oysters to "kissing the sea on the lips," he was speaking for his countrymen and their culinary courtship with oysters. Dedicated oyster farmers nurture bivalves along 2,000 miles of France's coastline in beds that have been cultivated since Roman times. For the French, oysters are a Christmas tradition and a year-round national obsession.

As soon as Brasserie Brightwell immigrated to the Eastern Shore, locals simply said "oui" and welcomed the fusion of Chesapeake oysters dressed up in French cuisine. The charming bistro houses a shucking station next to its open kitchen and presents a fine selection of regional bivalves.

During a recent visit, Barren Islands, Chincoteagues and Choptank Sweets were written on the raw bar chalkboard along with Virginia topneck clams and Maine lobster salad. The wood-fired grill churns out oysters baked with garlic and bread crumbs, grilled with fennel and parmesan cheese, and fried with caper aioli.

Brasserie Brightwell is a lovely place that balances European grace within a casual setting. Inside, cream-colored walls are adorned with vintage French cabaret posters, and the wooden bar is loaded with wine and aperitif bottles. Local craft beers are on tap. On a warm summer evening, the brick patio's red umbrellas and full-service bar offer a remarkably pleasant space for outdoor dining.

The menu reads like a classic French café with a nod to fresh local seafood. Tender steamed mussels come with pommes frites, and the cook masterfully grills whole trout and wild salmon. Meat lovers can get their fill with steaks, chicken, burgers and lamb sliders.

Washington Street Pub
& Oyster Bar

20 North Washington Street
Easton, MD 21601
(410) 822-1112
www.washingtonstreetpub.com

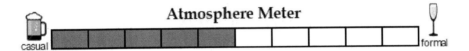

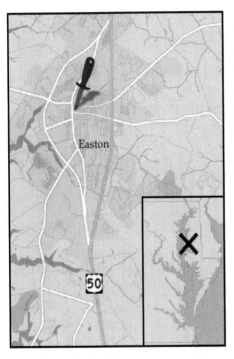

Eating oysters at Washington Street Pub is a testament to oyster houses' versatility and proves that a dozen on the half shell taste just as good at a cozy neighborhood bar as they do at a high-end restaurant. Sometimes even better.

At this pub, you can watch the Ravens or Redskins on flat-screen TVs with buddies at the bar while tossing back bivalves and washing them down with 20 draft beers ranging from Dogfish Head to Yuengling.

In autumn and winter, you can review a nice selection of oysters from Maryland and Virginia as well as brands from across the country. On a recent trip, Choptank Sweets were the local pick, which stood up quite well in taste tests against

Blue Points from Connecticut, Gold Creeks from the Pacific Northwest and Malpeques from Canada's Prince Edward Island. Littleneck clams from Virginia's Eastern Shore were delivered for slurping or steaming.

The oyster bar showcases Oysters Cordon Bleu baked with prosciutto and bleu cheese, rope-grown mussels steamed in creamy garlic broth with chorizo and tomatoes, and shrimp boiled in beer and Old Bay. Classic oyster stew and Maryland crab soup take the chill off a cold windy day. Crab cakes, lamb shepherd's pie and bangers with hash are outstanding.

Washington Street pub has a turn-of-the-century feel with exposed brick walls and vintage light fixtures. Two levels of seating stack a tier of tables above a floor lined with cozy booths. The atmosphere is upbeat and fun. The location, in the hub of downtown Easton's market square and across from the Talbot County Courthouse, makes strolling around this quaint town after a hearty meal a must-do activity.

The Eastern Shore

Jimmie & Sook's Raw Bar & Grill

527 Poplar Street
Cambridge, MD 21613
(410) 228-0008
www.jimmieandsooks.com

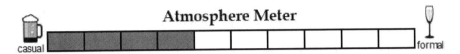

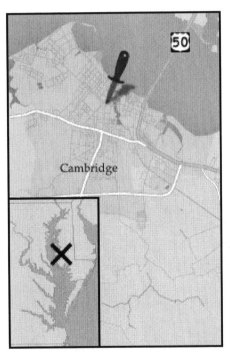

All around the Bay, Chesapeake watermen and residents refer to male crabs as "jimmies," and the lady crustaceans are called "sooks." So, when you see a restaurant named after crab genders, you know you're in for authentic seafood. The dedicated shucker standing at the raw bar placing half-shell oysters on platters covered with ice is another indication that Jimmie & Sook's believes in serving the local catch.

The raw bar choices are solid. Most of the oysters are pulled from local waters, and Choptank Sweets were featured on a recent visit. Also on deck were mussels steamed in wine with garlic, littleneck clams, cherrystones from Virginia, snow crab legs and steamed shrimp. A steamer pot combines them all into a platter that would make Neptune proud.

It's the go-to place to experience a genuine taste of Maryland Eastern Shore cuisine. Fried oysters, shrimp and calamari are light and crispy. Crab takes a commanding position on the menu, with imperial tucked into local treasures such as stuffed rockfish and chicken Chesapeake. Crab cakes are plump, and scallops with risotto are delicious. Baby back ribs, pineapple-braised pork shank, chicken pot pie and green peppercorn-encrusted tenderloin are among the meat-eaters' favorites.

The restaurant interior is decorated with working tools used by local watermen, and photographs on the walls present a visual history of the region. It's located in the center of Cambridge on a charming street lined with old trees, specialty shops and lively pubs. On the restaurant's front porch is a row of wooden rocking chairs that help slow down life's hectic pace for a while. An outdoor patio, plush with potted plants and herbs, offers a sweet escape for an evening. Live bands play on weekends.

Ocean Odyssey Restaurant

316 Sunburst Highway
Cambridge, MD 21613
(410) 228-8633
www.toddseafood.com

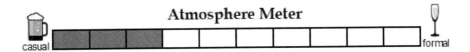

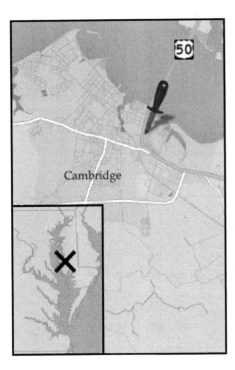

It's hard to miss Ocean Odyssey when you're driving into Cambridge. It's located in a commercial strip on Route 50 near the long bridge that spans the Choptank River. The one-story building's roof is painted bright orange, and its outdoor crab and beer garden is sure to catch your attention. Palm trees and colorful umbrellas stand above picnic tables. Beer cans are served in insulated coolers shaped like white watermen's boots. Yes, it is a boat load of fun.

Murals on the exterior walls commemorate the life of local watermen with depictions of their boats, crabs, fish and the Bay. It's a tribute to the restaurant's founding family who started in 1947 with a small crab factory and continues to produce crab meat under the label Bradye P. Todd & Son.

Crabs might be the traditional standard bearer for this place, but two other items are emerging to the forefront: oysters and beer. Choptank Sweets are the regular choice, often accompanied by Sewansecotts, Holy Grails, Barren Island Uglies and Chesapeake Golds. The selection is fresh, local and well-balanced between buttery and briny. Nine craft beers are on tap featuring local brews such as Dogfish Head, Jailbreak and Heavy Seas. Regulars suggest trying a bottle of Choptank, which is made by a Baltimore company called Brewers Art that designed this tasty ale especially for Maryland's Eastern Shore.

The rest of the menu reads like a fish lover's dream. The seafood combo combines crab cakes, shrimp and clam strips that are dusted with flour to order and flash fried. Mussels are steamed with beer, butter and herbs, while the "oyster shore boy" comes with lettuce and tartar sauce inside a warm bakery bun. Chicken wings, beef and bison burgers, and turkey sandwiches with gravy are made for carnivores.

Blue Point Provision Company

100 Heron Boulevard
Cambridge, MD 21613
(410) 901-6410
www.chesapeakebay.hyatt.com

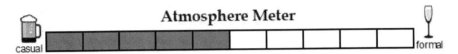

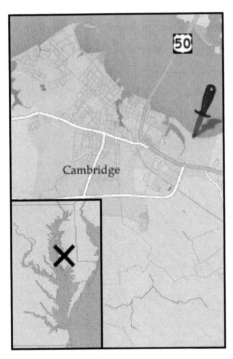

Nobody minds if Blue Point Provision's name sounds like a Connecticut oyster. And you'll hear no complaints about the restaurant's location at a Hyatt resort, especially if you like to relax and getaway in style while on a bivalve quest. What matters most is Blue Point's commitment to showcasing regional oysters and unique Eastern Shore cuisine.

This drive to serve local mollusks comes to a head in late November during Annual Oyster Week, when the staff pulls out all the stops to help guests discover and appreciate "the almighty oyster." Activities include cooking demonstrations by chefs on daily oyster dishes, beer and champagne pairings with a variety of oysters, and displays of Chesapeake oysters and marine life presented by Horn Point Oyster Hatchery.

Blue Point Provision's celebration of Bay oysters continues year-round with a dedicated shucker and reliable selection of bivalve brands from the area. Ordering Choptank Sweets is a slam dunk at the outdoor deck overlooking boats moored on the Choptank River. Other favorites tasted on a recent visit include Blue Points, Chesapeake Sweets, Chesapeake Golds and Chincoteagues. Fresh shucked oysters with spicy ketchup are the house specialty. Smoked oyster salad is a savory delight inside a crisp baguette, and broiled oysters offer a full flavor event topped with prosciutto and garlic herb cheese.

Other seafood delights include Maryland crab soup, mussels steamed in wine and herbs, fried flounder tacos and Cajun-style barbequed shrimp. Old Bay-rubbed Delmarva chicken, grilled skirt steak and smoked country ribs are standouts for the meat lovers. Add a casual upscale ambience and a panoramic view of the waterfront and you've found a lovely destination for indulging in the best of the Bay.

Brew River Restaurant

502 West Main Street
Salisbury, MD 21801
(410) 677-6757
www.brewriver.com

Atmosphere Meter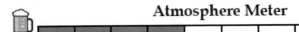
casual ———— formal

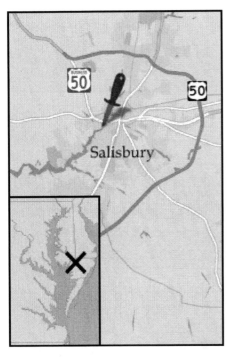

Brew River is located so far up the Wicomico River that you could throw an oyster shell from one bank to the other if you have a good arm. However, its outdoor dock bar and proximity to the marina in downtown Salisbury bring the zest of the Bay about 16 miles inland to this lovely town.

It opened in 2000 by a family that's been active in the restaurant scene since 1974 and also owns Harpoon Hanna's on Fenwick Island. That Atlantic connection forges a strong emphasis on regional seafood. The raw bar gathers fresh oysters from up and down the East Coast, and you can expect about three different bivalve brands each week. Chincoteagues, Blue Points and Massachusetts Salts were featured on a recent visit. Other regulars on the raw bar roster include Prince Edward Island mussels, littleneck clams and peel-and-eat shrimp. Happy Hour Buck-a-Shuck Oysters run from Monday to Saturday, and on Sunday you can indulge in $1 oysters all day long. Fried oysters and oysters Rockefeller are prepared flawlessly.

The all-you-can-eat special of snow crab legs, baby back ribs and fried chicken is a classic Eastern Shore feast. Local seafood is a menu mainstay with crab cakes, coconut shrimp and blackened scallops leading the charge. Steaks, burgers, pizza and chicken are on hand for meat eaters.

The atmosphere is casual, comfortable and buoyant. Pictures of Chesapeake crabs, oysters, watermen and boats hang from the restaurant's interior walls, and wooden barrels and hand-painted fish dangle from the rafters. An immense stone fireplace crackles during the winter. In the summer, the premium spot is outside on the expansive deck and lounge, where frozen cocktails cool guests on hot summer days and firepits radiate warmth when the seasons change.

The Eastern Shore

The Jackspot

6262 Marlin Street
Chincoteague, VA 23336
(757) 336-0512
www.thejackspot.com

Atmosphere Meter
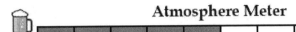
casual   formal

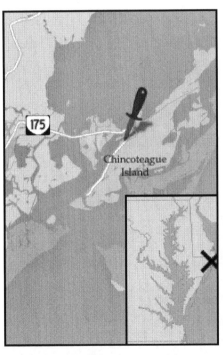

In the waters below the Route 175 causeway leading into Chincoteague float lines of oyster flats that serve as welcome wagons for what many consider a Mecca to briny bivalve lovers. This remote island is home to wild ponies and some of the world's finest oysters grown offshore by shellfish farmers such as Ballard, Tom's Cove and Toby Island. Pristine waters, glorious sunsets and spectacular scenery create an idyllic getaway destination.

Experts at oyster crawls of the region often recommend The Jackspot as a good starting point. It's located on the bayside of Chincoteague Island with a panoramic view of amber sea grass, soaring waterfowl and fishermen steering workboats through Black Narrow's waves. The Jackspot greets guests with a large waterfront island area, complete with palm trees swaying among bright blue and yellow umbrellas and picnic tables nestled in the sand. Sipping on house libations such as the spiced rum Saltwater Cowboy or Key Lime Crush activates a laid-back, on-vacation feel.

At this restaurant and others on the island, you won't find long lists of oyster brands from the Atlantic seaboard. When local oysters are such a premium commodity, folks prefer to stick with ones harvested close to home. But ask the server where your oysters were grown so you can taste the subtle flavor differences between the unique coves and farms.

A dozen fresh-shucked oysters in this setting is heavenly, and the menu presents options for those who prefer their bivalves cooked. Oysters Jackspot is a savory treat with bacon, spinach, shallots and heavy cream. Fried clam strips are garnished with a mustard tartar sauce. Oyster po' boys come in a toasted potato roll, and pan-roasted day boat scallops are spiced with aged chorizo. Local seafood drives the rest of the dishes. Burgers and chicken are also available.

AJ's on the Creek

6585 Maddox Boulevard
Chincoteague, VA 23336
(757) 336-5888
www.ajsonthecreek.com

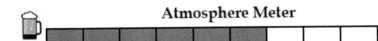

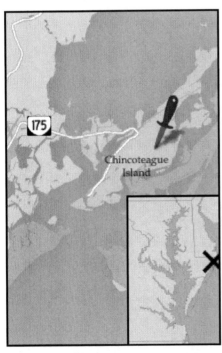

AJ's on the Creek is the type of place you hope to discover when heading out for a nice evening at the shore. White linen tablecloths, dark wood and cream-colored walls create a more upscale ambience than most of the places in this beachside town. Musicians singing to acoustic guitars lighten the mood, and seating on a screened porch overlooking the creek's marshy grasslands brings a casual atmosphere to warm summer nights.

It's a regional gem with an endearing back story about generations of a local family working hard in the kitchen. The place is named after Anthony J. Stillson, a jazz pianist and architect who founded the restaurant. Since 1985, his two daughters have managed the operations. One of them is married to a fisherman who brings his daily catch to her door.

Recipes have been handed down for generations and display the culinary finesse of cooks who live on the island and know how to draw the best from local ingredients.

All the oysters served here are grown in Chincoteague's bay, inlets and Atlantic waters. On the half-shell, these briny bivalves hit a world-class level of saltiness and plump texture. House specialties include oysters fried to a delicate crisp or blanketed and baked in a cream champagne sauce with sliced scallions and bacon crumbles.

The menu also presents traditional Chincoteague seafood that is authentic and fresh. The shellfish bouillabaisse is a melting pot of oysters, clams, mussels, scallops and shrimp in a garlic seafood broth that demands a good chunk of bread to scoop up every drop. Crab is fried into golden brown cakes or lightly mixed with mornay sauce in a creamy crab imperial. Meat eaters can opt for veal, steak, lamb chops or chicken.

The Village Restaurant

6576 Maddox Boulevard
Chincoteague, VA 23336
(757) 336-5120
www.chincoteague.com/thevillage

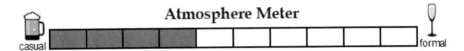

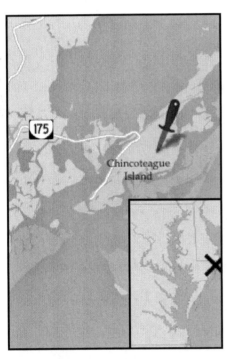

For about 38 years, The Village Restaurant has rustled up hearty seafood caught by mid-Atlantic fishermen. Family-run and family-friendly, this long wooden building stands along Eel Creek offering visitors a spectacular waterfront view of the region's plush marshlands.

Mother ducks and their little chicks paddle around in the water beneath the outdoor deck. The interior's cheerful red curtains, round wooden chairs and quaint nautical décor project a homey and welcoming feel.

The menu heralds a medley of seafood pulled from nearby waters. Chincoteague oysters and clams are shucked to order on the half shell or steamed to a plumb tenderness. Oyster stew is a creamy liquid gold. Oysters Rockefeller and

Clams Casino spearhead the cooked dishes, and shrimp are slowly barbequed to bring out their sweet ocean flavors.

Local crabs join the ranks with other edible sea creatures and make their mark stuffed into heirloom tomatoes or fried into chubby cakes. You can choose to have flounder and scallops fried, broiled or blackened, and the servings are always plentiful. Steaks, veal, chicken and pasta are available; desserts such as bourbon pecan pie and hot molten lava cake are simply irresistible.

The Village is located on a road with standard beach town attractions such as a mini golf course, bait and tackle shop, and souvenir stores. But a short distance away is the Museum of Chincoteague Island, a place that every oyster lover must visit. Its exhibits unveil a regional history of the half shell and explain how oysters played a role in America's growth from the early settlers to today's seafood industry. The extensive collection of vintage oyster cans is remarkable.

Oyster Farm Seafood Eatery at Kings Creek

500 Marina Village Circle
Cape Charles, VA 23310
(757) 331-8660
www.theoysterfarmatkingscreek.com

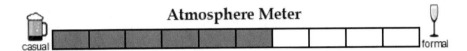

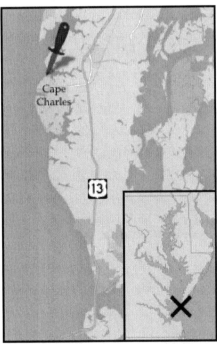

It's not unusual to sit on the gorgeous deck at Oyster Farm Seafood Eatery and watch ships cruise through the waves. But it's an extra bonus — and rather exciting for oyster fans — to see a boat coming around the bend and dumping piles of oyster shells into the water.

You feel like a witness to the inauguration of oysters that will eventually rest upon an icy tray at your table. That's because the restaurant is in the process of building its own aquafarm to produce boutique bivalves for its customers. It's part of private resort that celebrates a water-to-table dining experience where you can learn about the oyster-growing process and even harvest a bunch from the water. It's among the destinations listed on the Virginia

Oyster Trail and located north of the Chesapeake Bay Bridge Tunnel on the Eastern Shore.

The restaurant's oyster bar features bivalves from both the bayside and seaside. During a recent trip, the oyster list read like a veritable Who's Who of Bay aquafarms — Ruby Salts, Sewansecotts, Watch House Points, Misty Points, Indian Rocks and Cherrystones — to name a few. The shucker will do the heavy lifting and open your picks, or you can get a bushel of Kings Creek Salties to enjoy at home.

The menu at this stunningly beautiful location presents a splendid array of local seafood. Raw bar clams, oysters Casino or Rockefeller, PEI mussels provençal and cast iron seared scallops are among the favorites. Crab cakes and fried oysters represent Chesapeake classics, while Thai shrimp and Dragon Tuna with wasabi introduce new flavors to the Bay. When your meal is done, check out the massive fish tank in the dining room that's filled with creatures of the sea.

Washington, DC

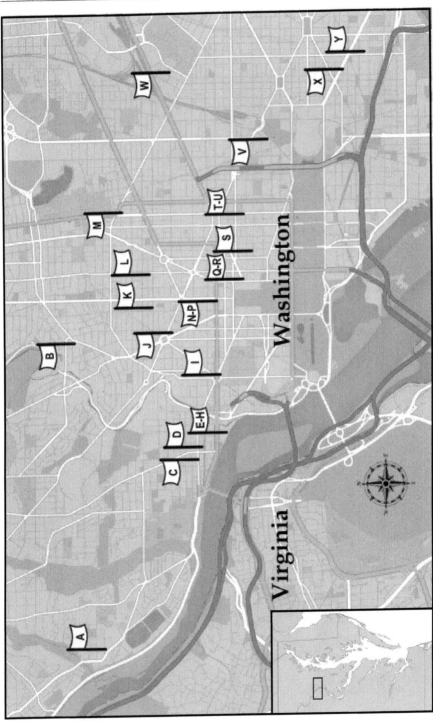

Washington, DC

- Ⓐ BlackSalt Fish Market & Restaurant 150
- Ⓑ Pop's SeaBar 152
- Ⓒ J. Paul's 154
- Ⓓ Sea Catch Restaurant & Raw Bar 156
- Ⓔ Fiola Mare 158
- Ⓕ Orange Anchor 160
- Ⓖ Tony and Joe's Seafood Place 162
- Ⓗ Sequoia 164
- Ⓘ District Commons 166
- Ⓙ The Gryphon 168
- Ⓚ Hank's Oyster Bar Dupont Circle 170
- Ⓛ Pearl Dive Oyster Palace 172
- Ⓜ Eat the Rich 174
- Ⓝ McCormick & Schmick's Washington 176
- Ⓞ P.J. Clarke's DC 178
- Ⓟ Catch 15 Restaurant & Oyster Bar 180
- Ⓠ Joe's Seafood, Prime Steak & Stone Crab 182
- Ⓡ Old Ebbitt Grill 184
- Ⓢ Oceanaire Seafood Room Washington 186
- Ⓣ Legal Sea Foods Restaurant & Oyster Bar
    Washington 188
- Ⓤ Clyde's of Gallery Place 190
- Ⓥ Johnny's Half Shell 192
- Ⓦ Rappahannock Oyster Bar 194
- Ⓧ Hank's Oyster Bar Capitol Hill 196
- Ⓨ Senart's Oyster & Chop House 198

BlackSalt Fish Market & Restaurant

4883 MacArthur Boulevard, NW
Washington, DC 20007
(202) 342-9101
www.blacksaltrestaurant.com

Atmosphere Meter

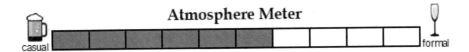

casual — formal

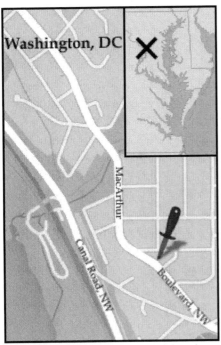

Black Restaurant Group has become the Poseidon of Washington seafood. Its family of restaurants, which includes Republic, Pearl Dive Oyster Palace and Black's Bar & Kitchen, is fanning out its tentacles across the metro region and becoming a beloved network of hot spots for oyster aficionados.

Each restaurant seems to fit perfectly into its location, and BlackSalt is no exception. Its subtle storefront easily blends in with the Palisades neighborhood's tall oak trees, bungalow houses and playgrounds filled with families. The Saturday farmer's market next door compliments BlackSalt's fish market that presents a cornucopia of seasonal, sustainable and irresistible treasures from the sea.

If you can bypass the alluring seafood display, you'll discover the restaurant's charming dining room with hand-painted murals of ocean life, soothing décor and welcoming atmosphere. Oyster lovers who want to get up close to the action take a seat at the bar in front of an icy bivalve station. Knowledgeable shuckers are eager to help guests who are just starting to dip their toes into the oyster scene.

Usually six to eight brands are featured, and they're split into local boutique oysters and premium imports that cost more per dozen. On a recent visit, homegrown Chesapeakes included Barren Island (MD) and War Shore, Sewansecott and Old Black Salt (VA). Oysters grown beyond the Bay's waters were Cotuit and Washburn (MA), Fisher's Island (NY), and Belon (ME). Oysters Rockefeller come with bacon, spinach and chive aioli. The rest of the menu is designed to offer a total seafood experience, complete with six types of caviar, mussels steamed five ways and enough shrimp, crab cakes, tuna and rockfish to make you want to return for more.

Pop's SeaBar

1817 Columbia Road, NW
Washington, DC 20009
(202) 534-3933
www.popsseabar.com

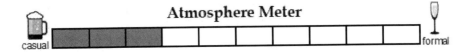

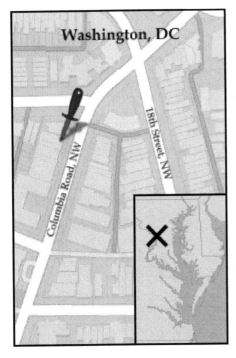

Oysters do not need to be pretentious, formal or stuffy, and they don't always appear at establishments where patrons are scared to speak above a whisper. No, today's Bay oysters are encouraged to be casual and even raucous, and they're served in places where we don't need to wear pressed shirts or spend a fortune to enjoy good oysters.

This concept took hold in September 2014 in Adams Morgan when Pop's SeaBar arrived on the scene. It calls itself a "boardwalk-inspired seafood bar" and replicates the carefree places that made going to the beach fun as a kid.

The restaurant captures a throwback diner vibe with a long central bar, aluminum stools with cherry red seats and vintage signs that proclaim the virtues of drinking cold beer and eating fresh seafood. Nautical artwork on brick walls underscores a crab shack theme. The upbeat atmosphere moves to additional upstairs seating and flows out to the patio where cooks are known to toss plump oysters on the grill and slather them with paprika butter.

Its more serious big-sister restaurant, Cashion's Eat Place, is next door, but Pop's is allowed to stay up late, until about 2:00 a.m. on weekends. Whether you stop by for an easy lunch or are among the hungry revelers hiking home on Columbia Road after a pub crawl night, you're certain to find plenty of good seafood here.

The raw oyster selection is impressive and presents an array of brands from Maryland and Virginia's shores. Big Bay oysters are flash fried to a golden crisp and placed on platters or on top of beef patties with coleslaw and pickled hot peppers. Peel-and-eat shrimp, fried smelts, Maryland crab cakes, and crunchy calamari are among the seafood favorites. Piping hot boardwalk chicken with Jersey Shore sauce will rekindle memories of ignoring your mom's warnings about applying sunscreen often. Special house cocktails, such as the Hup Hup Orange Crush or the Jungle Bird with rum, pineapple and lime, will conjure up images of a fun beach vacation.

J. Paul's

3218 M Street, NW
Washington, DC 20007
(202) 333-3450
www.jpaulsdc.com

Atmosphere Meter

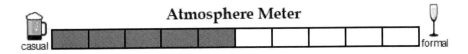

casual — formal

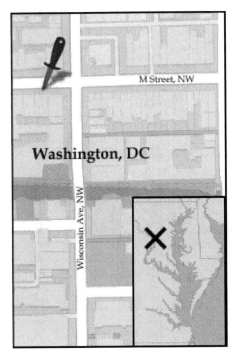

At the top of J. Paul's building is a tan brick noting the year 1898 when this lovely shotgun saloon was erected. Down at street level is a window display of oysters on ice that's enticing enough to interrupt the relentless flow of pedestrians on M Street. People stop and stare like kids at a candy store, and a bounty of bivalves lures them inside.

On the right side of this turn-of-the-century tavern is a stunning century-old mahogany bar that was once housed in a grand saloon at the Chicago stockyards. In the back dining room hang an exquisite pair of vintage elevator doors from New York's Waldorf Astoria, and brilliant blue and gold murals encircle the sky roof. It's a time traveler's fantasy back to the late 1800s when Chesapeake oysters were shipped around the globe as a precious culinary commodity.

For the past 30 years, J. Paul's has upheld the tradition of serving fine oysters and seafood from the East Coast. On a recent visit, the raw bar was packed with White Stone oysters and littleneck clams from Virginia, Blue Points from Connecticut, Malpeques from Prince Edward Island, and Old Bay spiced shrimp steamed in the house amber ale.

The bar area's atmosphere is so lively, especially when local football and baseball teams are on TV, that sitting at a tall wooden bar table and nibbling on oysters and seafood snacks provides plenty of entertainment. Fried oysters, clams steamed with white wine, butter and shallots, and ahi tuna tacos with spicy Asian slaw fit the bill nicely.

A calmer casual ambience presides over the dining rooms where more substantial entrees are served. Crab cakes are legendary, fish and chips are beer battered crispy, and grilled blackened salmon comes with garlic mashed potatoes. Burgers, fried chicken, steaks and ribs are also available.

Sea Catch Restaurant & Raw Bar

1054 31st Street, NW
Washington, DC 20007
(202) 337-8855
www.seacatchrestaurant.com

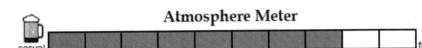

Atmosphere Meter — casual to formal

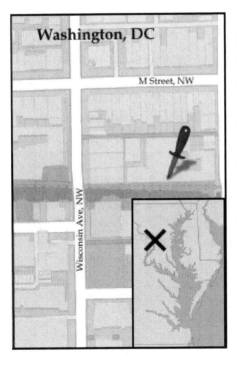

Locals would prefer that Sea Catch remained one of Georgetown's best kept secrets, but it's hard to keep quiet about this charming restaurant. Its discrete entry on M Street only posts a simple sign near a brick archway. Passing through it leads to a spacious courtyard with orange umbrellas and large planters overflowing with bright seasonal flowers.

The restaurant building dates back to 1842 when it served as a shipping warehouse for barge traffic on the C&O Canal. A long wooden deck overlooks this notable waterway, and a replica barge near the hostess stand pays tribute to its history. The interior décor uses gentle lighting to highlight centuries-old framework of stone and brick walls and ceilings of thick wooden beams. White linen tablecloths and a gray stone fireplace set the mood for a special evening. The atmosphere is romantic but not stuffy, and oysters are on their best behavior.

A 31-foot white marble bar creates a grandstand for stylishly sampling farm-raised oysters, mussels, clams, shrimp and house-smoked salmon. During a recent trip, the shucker presented trays of Virginia's Chincoteague oysters, as well as Kumamoto, Maple Point, and Dabob Creek from Washington State and Kusshi and Chef Creek from British Columbia. Oyster ceviche tops half shells with fresh tomatoes, cilantro and lime juice, and oysters Rockefeller heats them up with garlic, spinach and sweet cream.

The rest of the menu would make Poseidon proud. Seafood highlights include Tom's Cove Littleneck Clam Linguine, whole Maine lobster and bouillabaisse chocked full of fishy delights. Steak and chicken are also available.

Fiola Mare

3050 K Street NW
Washington, DC 20007
(202) 628-0065
www.fiolamaredc.com

Atmosphere Meter

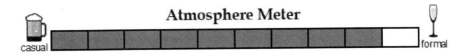

casual — formal

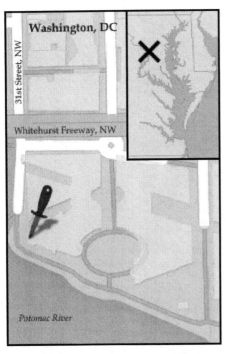

Georgetown Waterfront has undergone many changes since its time as a commercial wharf. Plans to develop the area began in the 1960s, and today's residents reap the rewards of that work. What was once a dusty parking lot beneath a rusty freeway on K Street has turned into a rolling green space with a cooling fountain, shade structures and a landscaped trail along the Potomac River.

Overlooking this bucolic urban renewal is a relatively new restaurant called Fiola Mare. Its commitment to serving fresh local ingredients with a Mediterranean twist is equal to its affinity for oysters. The gourmet raw bar selection includes East and West Coast oysters, middleneck clams, wild mussels, head-on prawns, Maine lobster, ahi tuna and sea urchin. Chesapeake oysters come and go with the seasons, but you can expect to find clean and melony Shigokus oysters from Washington State, delicate and briny Beau Soleils from New Brunswick, and briny and coppery Belons from Maine. Half shells topped with caviar is a decadent flavor adventure.

In this beautiful and breezy establishment, grilled steak is the main option for carnivores, but the menu is swimming with well-prepared seafood dishes. Wild Spanish monkfish with mussels and littleneck clams in an oregano tomato broth is exceptional, and Dover sole is filleted at your table. Sea scallops are simply grilled with olive oil and lemon, and ahi tuna carpaccio with olives and trout roe is divine.

Fans of classic drinks find kindred spirits at the main bar sipping craft cocktails such as Bee's Knees, Moscow Mule and Old Fashioned. The smaller and more casual Piccolo Bar is home to monthly Speakeasy Nights, which celebrate libations from the Prohibition Era.

Washington, DC

Orange Anchor

3050 K Street NW
Washington, DC 20007
(202) 802-9990
www.orangeanchordc.com

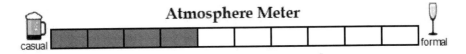

Atmosphere Meter: casual — formal

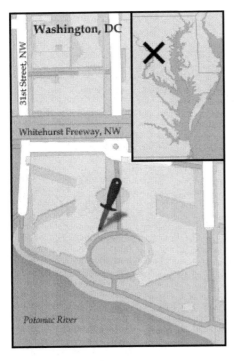

From the moment Orange Anchor docked at Georgetown Waterfront in 2014, it sent a message that the staff gives a shuck about Chesapeake seafood. It celebrated National Oyster Day with $1 bivalves all day long, ran Monday discount Oyster & Champagne nights through the summer, and hosted charity events for related local causes.

Happy hours are packed with Washington oyster enthusiasts as well as novices who get their toes wet in the bivalve scene with oyster shooters crafted from house-made Bloody Mary mix and Old Bay vodka.

Rappahannocks are the centerpiece of the raw bar, but other brands from Maryland, Virginia and the Atlantic Coast make cameo appearances depending on the season. Trays covered with oysters on ice come with cocktail sauce, mignonette, fresh shaved horseradish and grilled lemon. The shucker top off the half shells with champagne if you like.

Grilled oysters with parmesan cheese, parsley, butter and garlic go head to head with savory treats such as fried oysters breaded in cornmeal. Mussels come two ways: steamed in hard cider with bacon, bleu cheese and caramelized onion or in white wine with shallots and diced tomatoes. Crab meat fritters, seared rockfish and fried blue catfish show the cooks' Chesapeake roots. A unique seafood chili floats whitefish, salmon, shrimp and clams in a bubbling red stock.

The bright orange awnings make it easy to find this cheery eatery. Ropes are stretched between wooden pylons to mark off the patio. It's less formal than many of Georgetown's oyster houses with subtle nautical décor, a few buoys and oars hung on the walls, and a ship's steering wheel serving as the hostess station. And you can't beat the Potomac River view.

Washington, DC

Tony & Joe's Seafood Place

3000 K Street, NW
Washington, DC 20007
(202) 944-4545
www.tonyandjoes.com

Atmosphere Meter

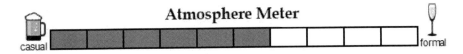

casual — formal

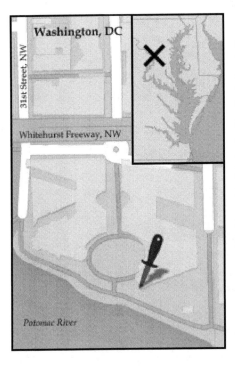

Many restaurants come and go at Georgetown Waterfront, but Tony & Joe's has been a staple here for decades. The location certainly helps, with stellar views of the Watergate, Kennedy Center, Roosevelt Island and Key Bridge just beyond your table. Its reputation for serving high-quality seafood attracts DC locals, politicians and tourists alike.

But Tony & Joe's is doing something special with oysters that's causing quite a buzz along the Potomac — they create exciting events with oysters to build a sense of community. During the summer, crowds flock to the Raw Bar Festival to sample the wares of regional aquafarms. In October, Tony & Joe's hosts the Shuck It! Beer & Oyster Festival that's one of the hottest tickets in town and features local bivalves, brews and musicians.

Chesapeake Oyster Lovers' Handbook

Recently, the restaurant began holding a fundraiser called Girls & Pearls to raise awareness about breast cancer and oyster recovery projects.

If you're not into crowds and prefer to go one-on-one with a plate of oysters, Tony & Joe's can accommodate your wishes. The raw bar menu lists a whopping 27 brands of oysters from across the country. Representatives of the Bay include Old Salt, Barren Island, Chesapeake Gold, Hollywood, Choptank Sweets, Stingray, Tom's Cove and Rappahannock oysters. Succulent broiled oysters are topped with spicy Tasso ham, spinach and parmesan cheese.

Plus, there's more in store for big seafood lovers. Topneck clams from Virginia and mussels from Prince Edward Island are standout starters. The Seafood Tower of lobster, oysters, clams, salmon, shrimp and crab showcases Neptune's favorite treasures. The Chesapeake Steam Pot simmers the local catch with sweet corn, tomatoes, potatoes and andouille sausage in Old Bay broth. Beef, lamb, chicken and pork are also available.

Sequoia

3050 K Street, NW
Washington, DC 20007
(202) 944-4200
www.arkrestaurants.com/sequoia

Atmosphere Meter

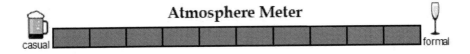

casual — formal

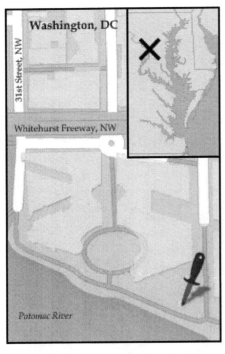

While it's refreshing to discover oysters in casual settings, there's a magical feeling that comes from sipping fine champagne and nibbling on a dozen at an elegant restaurant. And Sequoia certainly delivers dreamy upscale bivalves.

Regarded as one of Washington's most beautiful restaurants, the waterfront view at night is second to none. On the three-tiered veranda, you dine in style among trees wrapped in tiny white lights and let attentive waiters treat you like visiting royalty. The restaurant's interior, with floor-to-ceiling windows, classic nautical décor and long flowing white curtains, creates an enchanting and ceremonial ambience. It's a space designed for uptown weddings and special occasions.

North American oysters feel right at home amidst this grandeur. The raw bar features brands from the Atlantic and Pacific coasts, with Chesapeake bivalves gracing the menu on a regular basis. Chilled Seafood Towers erect an opulent display of oysters, mussels, clams, shrimp, lobster and crabs. Louisiana BBQ oysters are topped with pineapple, coriander relish and bleu cheese, while Bangs Island mussels are steamed in coconut milk. The Fisherman's Pot combines your favorite edible sea creatures in saffron tomato broth. Steaks, chicken, pork and salads round out the dining options.

Local history buffs like to note that the restaurant got its name from the official presidential yacht that was built in 1925. The glamorous ship ferried around players who changed American history. Herbert Hoover used it for fishing trips, John Kennedy celebrated his last birthday on board, and Richard Nixon used it to entertain Brezhnev on the waters. Today the yacht is docked downstream at a marina not far from the restaurant that bares it name.

District Commons

2200 Pennsylvania Avenue, NW
Washington, DC 20037
(202) 587-8277
www.districtcommonsdc.com

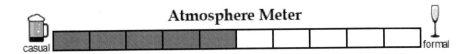

Atmosphere Meter

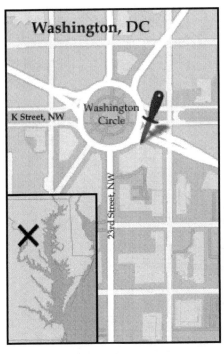

District Commons is located at Washington Circle, one of DC's complex traffic configurations that annoys local drivers and terrorizes tourists who try to navigate the mayhem in their cars. For pedestrians, it's a lovely green space in a bustling part of town energized by George Washington University's campus and medical center.

The front entrance to the restaurant looks like a standard steel-and-glass office building, but the outdoor patio acts as a sneak peek for an attractive restaurant inside. Spacious rooms with high ceilings sport a casual urban décor that is muted with unique light fixtures, brick interior walls, circular booths and floor-to-ceiling windows that let in rays of sunlight and provide an ideal stage for people watching. It's a new spin on the traditional American tavern and a welcoming port for oyster lovers seeking an alluring presentation of bivalves. In the center of the main dining room at the end of a long open kitchen stands the raw bar. The deep metal encasement filled with chilled seafood is set into the counter in front of a wood-burning oven. The visual contrast between ice and fire is striking and enticing.

The raw bar is a cool collection of seafood favorites — usually two or three brands of local oysters, wild Wellfleet clams, shrimp cocktail, crab meat and poached lobster — all deeply embedded in ice. Crispy fried oysters are accompanied by bleu cheese slaw. Blue Bay Mussels from Maine come in three patriotic colored sauces: red (red Thai curry), white (lemon thyme cream), and blue (bleu cheese, bacon and beer).

District Commons is under the corporate umbrella of Passion Food Hospitality, a local restaurant group that includes DC Coast, PassionFish and Penn Commons. The entrepreneurs behind these successful eateries also support charities such as Share Our Strength and Humane Society.

Washington, DC

The Gryphon

1337 Connecticut Avenue, NW
Washington, DC 20036
(202) 827-8980
www.thegryphondc.com

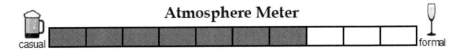

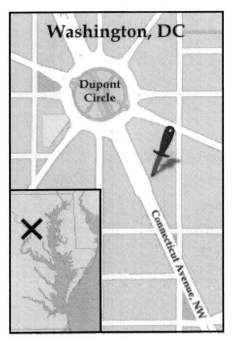

A mythical creature that is part lion and part eagle is called a gryphon. It's a fitting logo for a restaurant that brought a bold concept to Dupont Circle in May 2014. The founders, who also own Lost Society, have created a combination of steak house and raw bar with small-bite dishes designed for sharing among groups.

Oysters fit perfectly in Gryphon's collective dining experience, because the timeless ritual of splitting a dozen on the half shell with friends somehow makes bivalves taste better. At Gryphon you can mix and match brands to create an oyster sampling that covers the flavor spectrum from butter to brine. Tom's Cove Oysters from Chincoteague, Sting Rays from the Rappahannock River, Connecticut Blue Points, Washington State's Kumamotos, and Massachusetts Wiannos were on

Washington, DC **169**

hand during a recent visit. During happy hour Tuesday to Friday from 4:00 to 7:00 p.m., bivalve prices are cut in half to encourage exploring new types without busting your budget.

Middleneck clams, lobster and shrimp cocktail, and striped bass ceviche complete the raw bar round-up. Flash-fried oysters rest upon a uniquely delectable sauce of Worcestershire, smoked maple hot sauce and cilantro. Charred Portuguese octopus, crispy skinned Atlantic salmon and savory prosciutto-wrapped monkfish present a seafood lover's dream. Carnivores in the crowd are delighted by the offering of steaks, short ribs, burgers, lamb and surryano ham.

To top it off, all this remarkable food is served in a handsome, trendy dining space where oysters are prominently displayed in a long icy case at the entry. Dark wood and brick walls are accented with fantastic chandeliers, some of them made from antlers. On weekend evenings, DJs generate a night club vibe. Patient ladies room matrons dispense lipstick and hairspray to patrons, while oysters snap their shells in time to the music. It's an upbeat atmosphere that guarantees a good night out on the town.

Hank's Oyster Bar Dupont Circle

1624 Q Street, NW
Washington, DC 20009
(202) 462-4265
www.hanksoysterbar.com

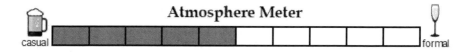

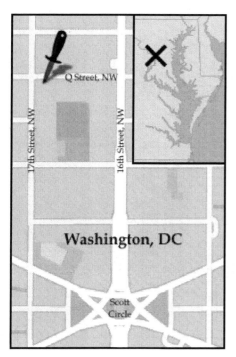

Exploring Dupont Circle is easier by foot than in a car. You don't have to deal with parking or traffic hassles, and you can set your own pace for strolling around this vibrant Washington neighborhood. You discover unique boutiques, galleries filled with colorful creations and elegant embassy buildings waving flags from around the world.

When your feet grow weary from hitting the streets, it's time to head over to Hank's Oyster Bar. Since 2005, this charming restaurant has been a favorite rest stop and watering hole for thirsty travelers. It's also become a major player in the DC oyster scene by adding locations in Capitol Hill and Old Town Alexandria, as well as hosting festivals to celebrate regional brews and bivalves.

Washington, DC **171**

When you visit Hank's, you can expect the chalkboard to display at least a half dozen oyster brands from the East and West Coasts. Cannon Cove (VA), HongaTonk (MD), Salt Pond (RI), and Washington State's Arcadia, Eld Inlet and Hood Canal oysters were featured during a recent trip.

The "Ice Bar" is overflowing with chilled choices, such as oysters, clams, shrimp and lobster. The Sake Oyster Shooter pours big Asian flavors into a tiny glass. You can sample a variety of bivalve dishes by sharing small plates including Hog Island style BBQ oysters, New England clam chowder or steamed blue mussels. Guests with hearty appetites dive into large plates packed with crisp fried oysters or Ipswich clams. Lobster deviled eggs and seared scallops with heirloom tomatoes are often washed down with a glass of Flying Dog Oyster Stout. Beef, pork and Chesapeake fried chicken complete the dining options.

Hank's success isn't just about exceptional seafood. Its casual atmosphere and soothing décor also contribute to being a choice destination. Warm weather guests can kick back on an outdoor patio shaded by trees. The lower-level lounge area and upstairs bar create intimate settings for a terrific dining experience.

Pearl Dive Oyster Palace

1612 14th Street, NW
Washington, DC 20009
(202) 319-1612
www.pearldivedc.com

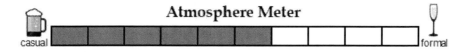

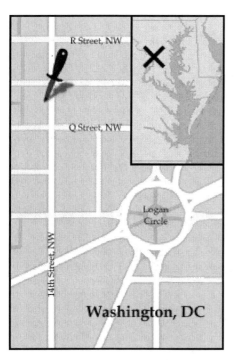

Finding a pearl in a Chesapeake oyster rarely happens. It's just not the way this species rolls. Instead, these bivalves are more interested in building firm plump muscles packed with big flavor. But if you're determined to discover a local jewel, visit Pearl Dive Oyster Palace.

Many elements of this Logan Circle hot spot come together to create one of DC's favorite oyster houses. The lovely urban rustic décor with exposed brick walls and a chandelier made of chains makes guests feel comfortable whether they're in dressy attire or jeans. In pleasant weather, the top half of the front entrance opens up to include outdoor patio seating at the bar. Upstairs at its sister restaurant, Black Jack, you can extend the evening with potent craft cocktails or a few games at the indoor bocce court.

Washington, DC **173**

Petite silver mermaids embedded in the marble bar top send a signal that the main attraction at Pearl Dive is the oyster. Near the back of the palace a shucker waits at his icy station ready to open your choice of shells. The daily list offers an impressive array of East and West Coast oysters such as Old Black Salts from Chincoteague, VA, Kumamotos from Washington State, Kusshis from British Columbia, and Cedar Islands and Beavertails from Rhode Island.

Hot oyster plates are the precious gems of the menu. Cornmeal crusted oysters with andouille sausage and sweet potato hash and grilled bacon-wrapped oysters are savory perfection. The Rockefeller is second to none. Crisp oyster po' boys, fried catfish, Creole seafood gumbo and crawfish etouffee show an affinity for Gulf Coast cuisine. Seafood dominates the rest of the dishes, and only a few options are on the table for carnivores: grass-fed hanger steak and an outstanding Pennsylvania Amish fried chicken dinner.

As an extra bonus, the bar sponsors events that bivalve aficionados don't want to miss. Roast 'n Toast in November entails oyster roasting, pig picking and glass clinking. Oyster and champagne tastings in December are nights to remember.

Eat the Rich

1839 7th Street, NW
Washington, DC 20001
(202) 316-9396
www.etrbar.com

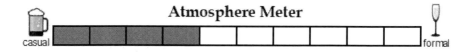

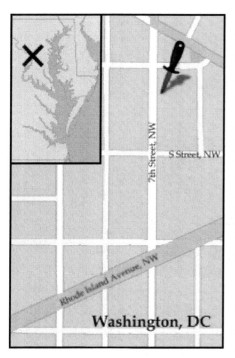

Eat the Rich breaks the mold of what people for centuries have envisioned as an oyster bar. It's a rock and roll bivalve stronghold that's the brainchild of Derek Brown (James Beard Award nominee and Chief Spirits Advisor for the National Archives) and Travis Croxton (owner of Rappahannock River Oysters and several oyster houses).

The concept comes from a mutual fondness for metal music, so the restaurant is named after a Mötorhead tune. Craft cocktails and Chesapeake oysters forge the keystone of a unique dining experience. The upbeat atmosphere is contagious, and the house song list is superb. Patrons mingle at a dark wood bar in a room with brick walls painted black and order canned beers, signature pitcher cocktails or crimson oyster shooters. Small tables stand near the front where devoted shuckers pop open shells. The main dining area abandons traditional seating and opts for long wooden benches and tables to encourage casual social meals. Metal aquafarm cages dangle from the ceiling.

Rappahannock River oysters are the headline act at the raw bar offering four distinct types ranging from buttery to briny: Rappahannocks, Sting Rays, Old Salts and Barcats. They are accompanied by chilled clams, wild Gulf prawns and Taylor Bay scallops. Redneck Laundry pairs trout roe caviar with Route 11 potato chips. Happy hour $1 oysters prove you don't have to be rich to eat like the rich.

The kitchen showcases Chesapeake Bay and mid-Atlantic seafood. Fried oyster sandwiches arrive with shaved cucumber and caper-chive remoulade, and swordfish swims with zucchini and tomatoes in a corn cream. Prawns nestle into Gruyere mac and cheese crowned with bread crumbs. It's deluxe comfort food made with fresh local ingredients.

Looking for more reasons to visit Eat the Rich? In October it hosts the World Food Day fundraiser to find smart solutions to hunger and poverty. Plus, you can attend a series of seminars here about the history of cocktails and spirits.

McCormick & Schmick's Washington

1652 K Street, NW
Washington, DC 20006
(202) 861-2233
www.mccormickandschmicks.com

Atmosphere Meter

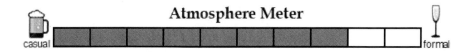

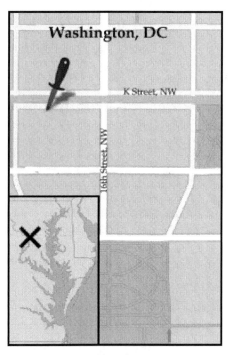

McCormick & Schmick's Washington is located right in the heart of the District's downtown commercial area, just a few blocks away from the White House and Lafayette Park.

The restaurant is surrounded by office buildings, which makes it a popular place to loosen up your tie after work and share happy hour oysters and seafood snacks with colleagues. The outdoor patio is a fine place to crack open a beer and give thanks for Fridays. During the week, the atmosphere is all about business talks. Tables are frequented by corporate types and government officials sealing deals in somber tones. On weekends, locals and tourists lighten the mood considerably.

Recent renovations have given the dining room a more modern décor than other M&S locations that sport an 1800s saloon vibe. Stained glass windows with gold, brown and gray geometric shapes match a similar pattern on the carpet, and amber silk curtains darken the room. A glass-enclosed case of bottles runs from the floor to the ceiling, highlighting an extensive wine collection.

The hushed room design serves as a perfect DC backdrop for sharing fresh-shucked oysters. Half shell specials during a recent visit included Blue Points from Connecticut, Malpeques from Prince Edward Island, Rappahannocks from Virginia, and Choptank Sweets from Maryland's Eastern Shore. Seafood standouts with a new twist on regional favorites: lump crab cakes with fire-roasted corn salsa, buttermilk fried shrimp with Chesapeake fries and parmesan-crusted flounder with butternut squash orzo. Steaks, burgers and chicken bring some turf to the surf for meat eaters.

Washington, DC

P.J. Clarke's DC

1600 K Street, NW
Washington, DC 20006
(202) 463-6610
www.pjclarkes.com/dc

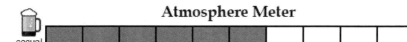

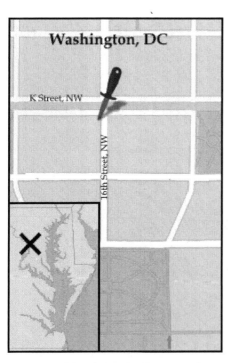

When P.J. Clarke's wanted to branch out beyond New York and establish a location in Washington, it came with gusto in 2010 right into the heart of downtown. Just a few blocks away from the White House, it's quickly become a watering hole for politicians, business leaders, journalists and lobbyists. The classic steak house has also emerged as a favorite gathering place for East Coast oyster enthusiasts.

Most of the bivalves that are blanketed in ice at the raw bar have traveled from Maryland, Virginia, New York and Rhode Island. The selection changes daily to offer the best and freshest from each region. A recent visit revealed an ample supply of oysters: Delaware Bays (NJ), Chincoteagues War Shores and Battle Creeks (VA) and Salt Ponds (RI). These briny delights were accompanied by chilled Maine lobsters and jumbo shrimp cocktail.

The large outdoor patio is a comfortable place to watch the eclectic parade of DC locals and visitors. Inside the restaurant, guests take a seat at tables covered with red and white checkered cloths. The dark wood-panel walls display portraits of U.S. presidents, and antique chandeliers hang from the ceiling. The atmosphere is business casual, and the kitchen is open until 1:00 a.m. for late-night snacks.

Waiters in long white aprons nod in approval at seafood selections. Fresh lobster rolls, Maryland lump crab croquettes, Gulf shrimp with grits and Ocean City fish tacos with avocado lime crème are on the menu's most wanted list. Distinctive side dishes, such as crisp parmesan tater tots and deviled eggs, make meals fun. Meat devotees enjoy plenty of choices among Black Angus steaks, burgers and chicken.

Catch 15 Restaurant & Oyster Bar

1518 K Street, NW
Washington, DC 20005
(202) 969-2858
www.catch15dc.com

Atmosphere Meter

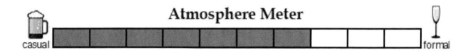

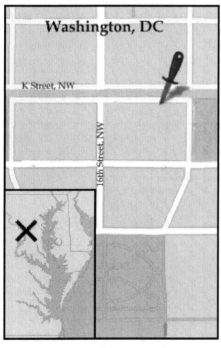

Every morning before many of us have poured our first cup of coffee, the chef at Catch 15 scours local markets to find quality seafood for his customers. Oysters are always on his mind, because this lovely Italian-influenced restaurant has become an urban haven for regional bivalve buffs.

Chesapeake Bay and East Coast oysters are featured here, and usually two or three brands run as daily specials. Misty Points and Blue Points from New England are popular selections. A dutiful shucker near the front of the house plucks them from their icy bed while spectators at the bar look on with eager anticipation. The raw bar is laced with aquatic pleasantries including shrimp cocktail, middleneck clams and lobster, plus a seafood tower that bundles them all with steamed mussels. Oyster shooters are crafted with peppered or citrus vodka.

The inviting outdoor patio beckons passersby to dine al fresco. Wide umbrellas are opened above wooden tables covered with white tablecloths, and black planters holding shrubs create a privacy barrier from the street. Three stools at the window, for lucky guests who can snag them, provide a view of the chic interior.

Soft lighting, cream-colored flowing curtains, rich wood paneling and thick cushioned chairs create a setting that makes you want to linger for hours. An impressive fine wine collection covers the walls.

Italian small plates lead the menu with seafood that fuses Mediterranean and American cuisines. Oysters are baked imperial with brie and lump crab meat or tempura-fried with a sweet and hot chili sauce. Garlic lovers relish clams casino and shrimp scampi. Main dishes show a preference for seafood, with standouts such as scallop and porcini risotto and a Sicilian stew simmering with a cornucopia of fresh shellfish. Meat dishes offer lamb, beef, veal and chicken. Pasta is made in house.

Washington, DC

Joe's Seafood, Prime Steak & Stone Crab

750 15th Street, NW
Washington, DC 20005
(202) 489-0140
www.joes.net

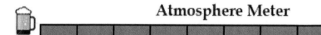 **Atmosphere Meter**

casual | | | | | | | | | | formal

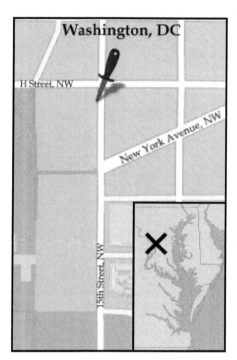

When Joe's Seafood rolled into town, it was greeted with great fanfare, because DC can't seem to resist fresh fish or big beautiful spaces. Joe's fit the bill on both accounts.

Just a stone's throw from the Treasury Department, this high-end restaurant is located in a former Union Trust Bank building. Gone are the bank tellers and deposit slips, replaced by shuckers and oyster lists. Gray marble columns, arched windows with sleek curtains and palm trees splashing color against beige walls establish an elegant dining décor. The enormous bar with a black granite countertop indicates a commitment to shaking classic cocktails for Washington's A-list. It's a large space with 475 seats, but waiters in tuxedos move smoothly between tables draped in white linens.

The original Joe's Stone Crab started in Miami Beach in 1913. In 2000, it partnered with Chicago-based Lettuce Entertain You Enterprises, and set anchor in the nation's capital in 2014. While the restaurant is best known for Key West stone crabs, icy trays of oysters have elbowed their way into the bar. The chef offers at least three brands that flow from buttery to briny tastes. Kumamoto (CA), Raspberry Point (PEI) and Sewansecott (VA) made the grade on a recent visit.

In keeping with the name, the menu is split between dishes from the sea and the land. Oysters Rockefeller and fried calamari appetizers are savory warm-up acts for colossal lump crab cakes and broiled seafood platters with lobster tail, shrimp and scallops. Signature prime steaks and double-cut lamb chops come with a high price tag and lots of flavor.

Old Ebbitt Grill

675 15th Street, NW
Washington, DC 20005
(202) 347-4800
www.ebbitt.com

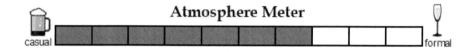

Atmosphere Meter

When you eat oysters at Old Ebbitt Grill, you get to experience a place steeped in local and national history. Built in 1856, it's DC's oldest saloon. It began as a boarding house where President McKinley once lived. Presidents Ulysses Grant, Andrew Johnson and Grover Cleveland were known to belly up to the graceful wooden bar.

Over the years, the turn-of-the-century saloon has amassed an extensive hoard of historic collectibles such as famous paintings, duck decoys, antiques and clocks. They're all on display, along with animal heads bagged by Theodore Roosevelt that hang above the main bar. Antique gaslights and English lace curtains complete the vintage vibe.

Oyster seekers appreciate the historic merit of Old Ebbitt's dining rooms, but real bivalve enthusiasts gravitate toward the side oyster bar. It's a narrow space where three to four shuckers stand shoulder-to-shoulder splitting open shells and placing them on ice-laden trays. They're in constant motion to keep up with the demand for thousands devoured each week.

Eight East Coast oysters are staples on the menu: Barnstable and Wellfleet (MA), Salt Pond (RI), Kusshi (BC), Navy Point (NY), Harpswell Flat and Permaquid (ME), and Sunberry Point (PEI). Local Chesapeake bivalves are mixed in regularly, depending on the season. Companions at the raw bar include littleneck clams, shrimp and crab claws.

Oyster adoration comes to a head once a year on the weekend before Thanksgiving at a raucous celebration called The Oyster Riot, where thousands of revelers eat bivalves and drink international wines. Tens of thousands of oysters are sacrificed for a good cause that benefits local musicians.

Washington, DC

Oceanaire Seafood Room Washington

1201 F Street, NW
Washington, DC 20004
(202) 347-2277
www.theoceanaire.com

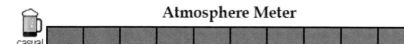
Atmosphere Meter
casual — formal

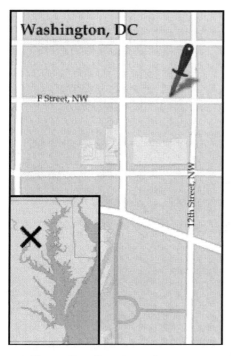

Can a restaurant be part of a huge corporation that owns over 500 properties and 40 brands (such as Chart House, Bubba Gump Shrimp Co. and McCormick & Schmick's) really deliver fresh local seafood? Yes, and it works surprisingly well at Oceanaire Seafood Room. Its parent company, Landry's Restaurants, started in 1980 as a fish eatery in Katy, TX, and has evolved into a conglomerate with high-end locations across America.

Its success could be attributed to having the corporate muscle to fly in fresh ingredients from around the world daily while making connections with regional growers and watermen. For instance, the oyster list touts six brands from Washington

State, Prince Edward Island, Connecticut and Massachusetts, yet it's balanced with a half dozen bivalves from Maryland and Virginia, including Choptank Sweets, Battle Creeks, Skinny Dippers and Chincoteagues. On Sundays, $1 local oysters are featured at the bar.

An upscale dining experience at Oceanaire can begin with caviar and end with Baked Alaska, and encompass schools of good seafood in between. The daily chalkboard promotes new arrivals from the sea, such as striped bass, tuna, Carolina red snapper and topneck clams. Raw bar regulars include house-cured Scottish salmon, crab meat cocktail and tequila shrimp ceviche. Murphy's Red Ale steamed mussels and oysters Rockefeller are delicious, and the hearty seafood bouillabaisse stews together shellfish in a spicy garlic broth. Steaks, chicken and pork are reserved for meat eaters.

Dishes are as artfully arranged as the dining room furniture. Large round ceiling fixtures radiate soft indirect light upon aqua blue circular booths. A few mounted trophy fish garnish the walls, creating a sophisticated nautical vibe. An extensive wine list adds to the special evening feel.

Washington, DC

Legal Sea Foods Restaurant & Oyster Bar Washington

704 7th Street, NW
Washington, DC 20001
(202) 347-0007
www.legalseafoods.com

Atmosphere Meter

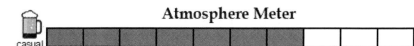

casual — formal

Plenty of restaurants offer daily or weekly oyster specials, but Legal Sea Foods' month-long oyster festival shows a mighty commitment to mollusks. For seven years running, this feast has gathered bushels of bivalves from Massachusetts, Canada, New York, Maine and Rhode Island and attracted crowds of fervent seafood fans from around the region.

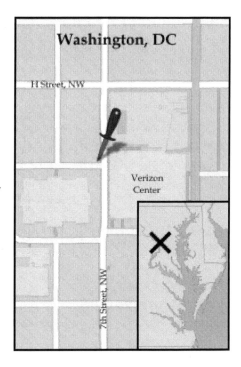

The oyster list feels like a Who's Who of East Coast favorites — Wellfleet, Malpeque, Kusshi, Naked Cowboy, Wianno, East Beach Blonde, Cotuit — to name a few. Deadrise, the fest's official drink, shakes up organic vodka with muddled cucumber, lime, and grapefruit bitters. Oysters on the half shell take center stage, but adding a little heat and unique ingredients creates some tasty dishes. Fried options include Buffalo oysters with bleu cheese and celery, BBQ oysters with cole slaw, sriracha oysters with Tasso ham and roasted corn, and fried oysters with eggs. It's hard to resist baked options such as lobster spinach oyster, crab and cheese oyster, and roasted oyster with smoked chorizo butter.

Since it arrived in the nation's capital in 1995, Legal Sea Foods has presented award-winning recipes for a gamut of aquatic creatures, and many of the festival dishes appear on the regular menu. It's part of a restaurant group that began as a family fish market in Cambridge, MA, in 1950 and has expanded to 35 eateries along the Atlantic seaboard from Virginia to Rhode Island. The Washington location is in Chinatown on a bustling street near the Spy Museum and National Portrait Gallery. An upbeat atmosphere fills three spacious rooms, and an open contemporary design creates a serene sanctuary for enjoying high-quality seafood.

Washington, DC

Clyde's of Gallery Place

707 7th Street, NW
Washington, DC 20001
(202) 349-3700
www.clydes.com/gallery-place

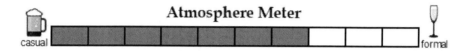

Atmosphere Meter

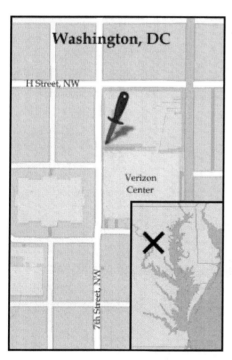

The entrance to Clyde's of Gallery Place serves as a reminder that we really should not judge a book by its cover. The circular black metal façade suggests that a somber mood awaits inside. Quite the opposite is true.

The restaurant's interior is big, bright and beautiful — a two-story modern rendition of a grand Victorian saloon. Elegant blonde woodwork is anchored by intricate mosaic tiles and accentuated with colorful paintings and statues. A stunning central staircase leads your eyes upward to high vaulted ceilings, and sunlight illuminates the four bars, five dining rooms and a raw bar.

It's located just steps away from the Verizon Center, DC's venue for hockey and basketball, so it makes sense that a sports theme has emerged. But the occasional splash of nautical artwork is a clue that an all-star lineup of oysters is warming up in the shucker's bull pen. Crowds of bivalve lovers are tempted to roar when they open an oyster menu with a wine-sipping mermaid on the cover. The daily roster calls up major players from along the East Coast, including Kusshi, Pemaquid, Salt Pond and Wellfleet. On deck at the raw bar menu are littleneck clams, Jonah crab claws, jumbo shrimp and lobster cocktail. Mermaid platters encourage you to recruit a few of each for a complete taste test.

Oyster Hour at the bars Sunday through Thursday cuts the prices in half, which energizes an already lively vibe. The regular menu is loaded with fresh local seafood. House specialties include lobster pot pie, baseball-sized crab cakes, cod croquettes with sriracha aioli and sesame crusted tuna with chilled soba noodles. Among the tasty selections for meat eaters are reubens and burgers, braised short ribs, Yuengling pork stew, and roasted brick chicken.

Johnny's Half Shell

400 North Capitol Street, NW
Washington, DC 20001
(202) 737-0400
www.johnnyshalfshell.net

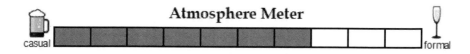

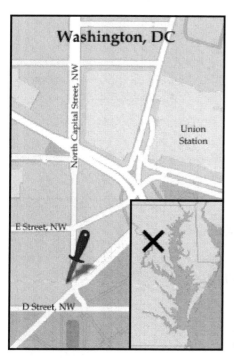

With Union Station conveniently located a few blocks away, there's no excuse for skipping Johnny's Half Shell while doing a Capital Hill oyster crawl. Lounging on the outdoor patio with a cool cocktail, nibbling on a plate of fresh oysters and savoring a stellar view of the capitol dome delivers the quintessential DC bivalve experience. Plus it's a lovely place with terrific food and a décor that proves oyster and fish art can be tastefully displayed.

 The restaurant's beige walls come alive with old family photos, framed oyster can labels, vintage porcelain oyster plates and a few mounted trophy fish. White linen tablecloths might suggest a formal environment, but jazz and blues music in the background keeps the vibe lively. The size of your group isn't a problem with three private dining rooms to accommodate larger parties.

Many oyster lovers prefer to sit at the bar. The ceiling is lined with white lights, and a fish tank doubles as a beer tap. You can lean your elbows on the white marble bar top, watch sea creatures swim through red coral and keep an eye on the shucker as he takes his knife to the shells. Usually two or three Chesapeake and East Coast oysters are offered, but the brands are rotated often so you have new types to try with each visit. Patuxent River oysters from Maryland and Massachusetts Wiannos were served at a recent oyster crawl.

Johnny's moved to this wonderful location in 2006 with the goal of preparing classic American seafood. Standouts include crispy fried oysters, plump Maryland-style crab cakes, sautéed sea scallops, grilled rockfish fillets, and a hearty Chesapeake bouillabaisse that simmers fish, shellfish and a mini crab cake in a rich lobster broth.

Rappahannock Oyster Bar

1309 5th Street, NE
Washington, DC 20002
(202) 544-4702
www.rroysters.com

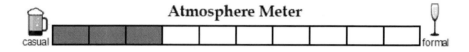

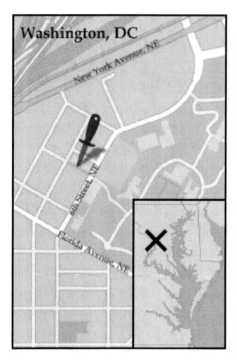

A tall map on the wall points out the locations of aquafarms that bring fresh bivalves to Rappahannock Oyster Bar. The menu's flavor descriptions of these brands have a direct link to where the oysters grow.

Here's how it works. Rappahannock River Oysters come from Topping, VA, where fresh water from the Blue Ridge Mountains pours into the Bay. Oysters here soak up water that is more fresh than salty, so they taste sweet and buttery. Stingrays live in Mobjack Bay, a cove that has a higher salinity level because it's closer to the mouth of the Chesapeake. That's why Stingrays have a mildly briny flavor. Old Salts, who lounge off the coast of Chincoteague, VA, absorb the Atlantic's salty seas and develop a bold briny attitude. This flavor concept isn't revolutionary. In fact, it's been around since the early Roman times. But what makes it new is the way the Rappahannock folks are integrating this idea into a 21st century model of producing and serving oysters that is sustainable and beneficial to the Chesapeake Bay.

To experience this in person, head over to historic Union Market, where Rappahannock Oysters Bar is surrounded by stalls of artesian cheeses, breads, sausages and more. These aquafarmers double as restaurateurs, who gladly shuck a sample platter with each oyster type and take you on a flavor journey from sweet to salty.

The staff is eager to answer questions about their oysters and recommend other dishes with bivalves that will energize your taste buds. Grilled oysters with smoked jalapeño butter are one step away from the pristine raw state by infusing a touch of heat into the brine. Oyster chowder is peppered with local bacon, the lambs and clams combo warms the heart, and crab cakes take a lighter turn with celery root slaw and remoulade. After you swipe the last morsel from your plate, you'll leave here with a greater appreciation for oysters.

Hank's Oyster Bar Capitol Hill

633 Pennsylvania Avenue, SE
Washington, DC 20003
(202) 733-1971
www.hanksoysterbar.com

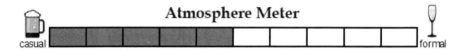

Atmosphere Meter — casual / formal

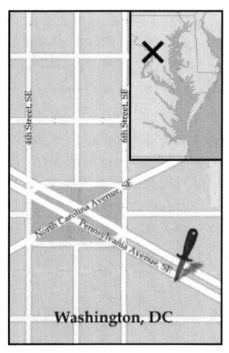

On Capitol Hill, where politicians are known to play powerful shell games under a big white dome, is Hank's Oyster Bar. It's a cozy place with such a congenial atmosphere that Democrats and Republicans put aside their differences and break bread over a platter of Chesapeake oysters.

This Hank's location is smaller than its sister restaurants in Dupont Circle and Old Town Alexandria, but the outdoor patio helps disburse crowds of hungry patrons during warm weather. Plus it provides a front-row seat for watching staffers, congressmen and lobbyists scurrying about and doing the people's business.

Once you step inside, attention shifts from politics to oysters, and debates focus on flavors rather than issues.

Hanging on the wall is a chalkboard that presents candidates from the East and West Coasts. On a recent visit, Virginia's representatives included James River, Tarkill Creek, Battle Creek and Salty Wolfe oysters. Washington State's bivalve nominees were Ayock Salt and Goose Point.

Every night from 10:00 p.m. to close, raw bar selections are reduced to half price. That gives more bang for your buck when sampling chilled oysters, middleneck clams, seafood ceviche with lime and jalapeño, and Old Bay peel-and-eat shrimp. The rest of the menu features coastal and New England beach favorites, such as lobster rolls, fried Ipswich clams, oyster po' boys and crab cakes. Dishes are well prepared, the staff is eager to please, and the vibe is lively.

The beer list presents an extensive array of ales, stouts and lagers, and craft cocktail names are enticing. It's hard to resist drinks called "Mommy Doesn't Get Drunk, She Just Has Fun" or "No. You Cannot Have This On The Rocks."

Senart's Oyster & Chop House

520 8th Street, SE
Washington, DC 20003
(202) 544-1168
www.senartsdc.com

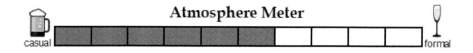

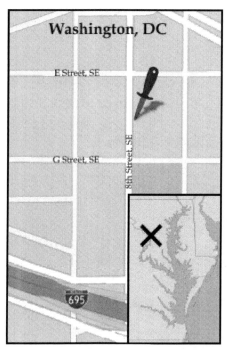

Senart's is a hidden gem that every oyster fan in Washington needs to visit. It's located in an up-and-coming area between Capitol Hill and the Navy Yard, just a stone's throw from bustling Eastern Market. Strolling around the neighborhood's turn-of-the-century row houses and taverns is like taking a step back in time.

The restaurant pays tribute to the city's history with photographs of DC's main attractions and monuments. Vintage pictures of oyster shuckers at their stations, watermen in drenched raincoats and waiters in long aprons honor the working folks who keep this town running.

Dark wood walls, dim lighting and leather booths indicate that you've entered a classic oyster and steak house. The ice and chrome raw bar holds a prominent position at the entry and is filled to the brim with bivalves from the East Coast. On a recent visit, Holy Grails and Hollywoods (MD), Malpeques and Raspberry Points (PEI), Blue Points (CT), and Wellfleets and Wiannos (MA) took center stage among chilled lobsters and lemons. Oyster brands are rotated on a weekly basis depending on the availability.

The chef does a splendid job of balancing dishes from the land and sea. If you're in the mood for surf, you can choose items such as fried oysters, New England clam chowder or salmon with risotto and spinach. Double-cut pork chops, juicy rib eye steaks and braised lamb shanks bring smiles to the faces of carnivores.

The atmosphere is casual and pleasant, as is the case with many of Senart's sister restaurants, including Hawk 'n' Dove, The Chesapeake Room and Boxcar Tavern. They're part of Barracks Row Entertainment, a local restaurant group.

200 Northern Virginia

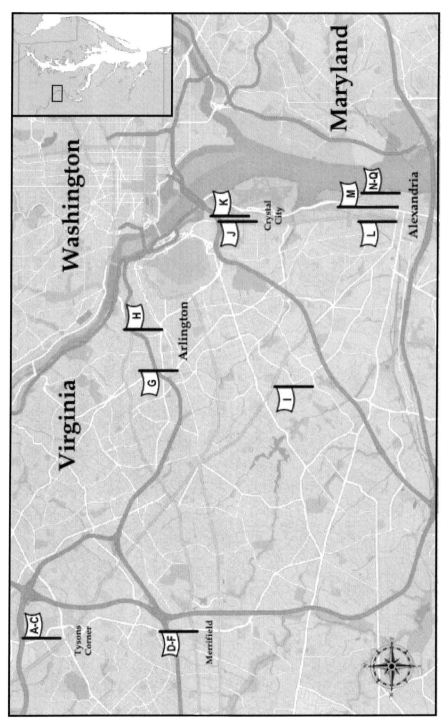

Northern Virginia

- Ⓐ McCormick & Schmick's McLean 202
- Ⓑ Clyde's of Tysons Corner 204
- Ⓒ Legal Sea Foods Restaurant & Oyster Bar McLean 206
- Ⓓ BRINE 208
- Ⓔ Sea Pearl Restaurant & Lounge 210
- Ⓕ Trio Grill 212
- Ⓖ Mussel Bar & Grille Arlington 214
- Ⓗ Lyon Hall 216
- Ⓘ Clyde's at Mark Center 218
- Ⓙ Legal Sea Foods Restaurant & Oyster Bar Arlington — Crystal City 220
- Ⓚ McCormick & Schmick's Arlington 222
- Ⓛ Hank's Oyster Bar Old Town 224
- Ⓜ Columbia Firehouse Restaurant & Barroom 226
- Ⓝ Overwood 228
- Ⓞ Blackwall Hitch Alexandria 230
- Ⓟ Fish Market Restaurant & Raw Bar 232
- Ⓠ Union Street Public House 234

McCormick & Schmick's McLean

8484 Westpark Drive
McLean, VA 22102
(703) 848-8000
www.mccormickandschmicks.com

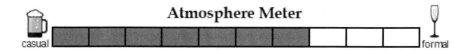

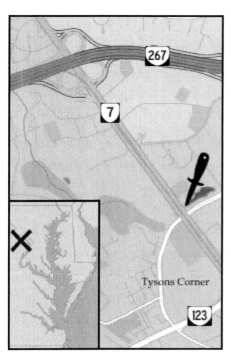

Gray suburban office buildings don't always set an attractive stage for eating oysters. But McCormick & Schmick's in McLean defies stereotypes about dull destinations and creates a fine-looking home for bivalves. From the minute you drive into the circular stone driveway and the valet attendant takes your keys, you feel like you've arrived at someplace special.

Black wrought iron furniture greets guests on the patio at the entrance. Inside, three spacious dining rooms are divided into privacy spaces with plush green curtains hung above wood-enclosed booths that look a bit like church confessionals. The McCormick and Schmick crests are etched into cut-glass windows, and vintage stained glass chandeliers are mounted on the ceilings. Muted inside voices feel more appropriate than raucous laughter.

The lounge area's old-fashioned saloon décor is accented with vintage artwork and a moose head mounted on the wall. Embedded in the long wooden bar top is where you find the oyster treasure trove. Encased in glass and metal, the icy bivalve nest is tended by busy shuckers. Chesapeake Golds, Chincoteagues and Rappahannocks were on tap during a recent visit. The Chef's Daily Oyster showcases regional aquafarms, and on Wednesdays at happy hour, oysters and shrimp prices are trimmed down to $1 each.

The regular menu reads like a fisherman's fantasy, and seafood shares the spotlight with fresh local ingredients. Standouts include skillet-blackened redfish with blue crab salsa, seared sea scallops with crab potato hash, and Jake's Famous Bouillabaisse loaded with king crab, shrimp, mussels, clams, fish and calamari. Beer-battered fish and chips comes with Chesapeake fries. Meat eaters can choose chicken or bump steaks and burgers to a new level with truffle butter and boursin bleu cheese on top.

Clyde's of Tysons Corner

8332 Leesburg Pike
Vienna, VA 22182
(703) 734-1901
www.clydes.com/tysons

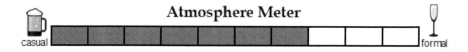

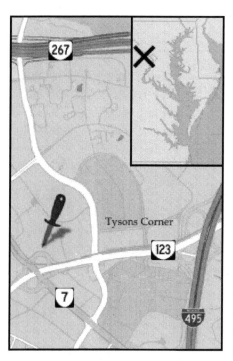

You never know what to expect when you enter a Clyde's location for the first time. Each one is uniquely decorated and establishes a personal style regardless of its surroundings. Clyde's at Tysons has a building with a low copper roof and an inconspicuous stone and brick entrance. A tall water tower hovers above it all.

A pair of elegant 1930s lampposts in front share the secret that dazzling Art Deco décor is waiting inside. It's a spectacular throwback to the Gatsby era when Chesapeake oysters, champagne and pearls were the bee's knees around the world. Four glamorous dining rooms are decked out in vintage furnishings and murals of bare-chested mermaids frolicking in the sea. Two palm trees flank a sleek fountain that was made in 1939 by the artist who designed Hollywood's Oscar statues.

Nibbling on oysters in this graceful setting is delightful, but Clyde's doesn't let the décor drive your dining experience. Oysters are plentiful, and an East Coast bivalve elite arrives at your table dressed up on shiny silver trays. On a recent visit, shuckers offered Barnstable, Cotuit, Salt Pond and Wellfleet from Massachusetts, along with Canada's Kusshi. Littleneck clams and shrimp join the chilly upper-crust raw bar. Sparkling and white wine pairings are suggested, but a grilled Bloody Mary oyster shooter with pepper vodka steals the show. Happy hour 50% discounts ensure everyone gets a bite.

Steamed mussels and crab towers are wonderful starters, and the American farmhouse cheese sampler leaves stomach space for a sumptuous seafood feast. Crab cakes and seared rockfish give a nod to Chesapeake cuisine, while grilled swordfish, sautéed salmon and battered fish and chips present the Atlantic Ocean's bounty. Burgers, chicken, steaks and sandwiches are on call for meat devotees.

Legal Sea Foods Restaurant & Oyster Bar McLean

2001 International Drive
McLean, VA 22102
(703) 827-8900
www.legalseafoods.com

Atmosphere Meter (casual — formal)

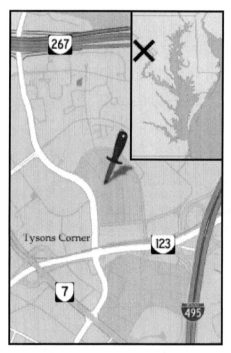

Legal Sea Foods' expanding restaurant empire now stretches down the East Coast from Rhode Island to Georgia. When its franchise dropped anchor in Tyson's Galleria, weary shoppers and oyster fans alike welcomed this soothing spot as a respite from the tangled net of retail stores, parking lots and new office buildings.

The double-decker restaurant, with entrances on both the first and second floors, has made its mark for serving fresh seafood from the Atlantic Ocean and oysters from the Eastern seaboard. On a recent visit, raw bar choices included Wellfleets, Merrys, Sandy Necks and Wiannos from Massachusetts and creamy Kusshi oysters from British Columbia. The lofty Seafood

Northern Virginia

Tower presents a chilled assortment of shellfish that includes oysters, shrimp and clams. A special dish of oysters baked with spinach, cheese and bits of lobster is applauded as savory one-bite wonders. Fried Buffalo oysters with bleu cheese stir up a bivalve bonanza.

The menu offers much more surf than turf. Fresh catch classics: New England fried clams, lobster bake, Portuguese fisherman stew, and sautéed shrimp with garlic, tomato sauce and housemade pasta. Landlubbers are limited to hanger steaks and barbeque ribs.

The décor exceeds shopping mall expectations with an uncluttered contemporary design. Charming blue and white tiles are laid into warm cherry wood panels, and black leather benches with delicate white pinstripes line the windows. Large trophy fish are mounted on the walls near an open show kitchen. The spacious bar upstairs provides a safe port for sipping cocktails and waiting for rush hour traffic to abate.

BRINE

2985 District Avenue
Fairfax, VA 22031
(703) 280-1000
www.brinerestaurants.com

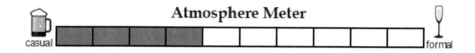

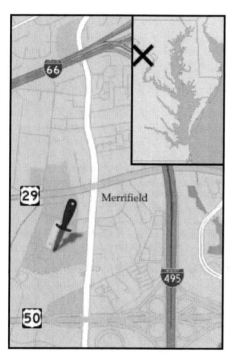

During the late 1990s, the Chesapeake oyster population plummeted to historic lows due to disease, overfishing and pollution. In 2001, amidst this gloomy era, cousins Travis and Ryan Croxton took over their family's 150-year old oyster leases in coastal Virginia.

Rejecting old harvesting methods, such as dredging that destroys oyster habitats, they turned to new sustainable aquaculture techniques to resurrect local bivalves. Fast forward about 15 years and the Croxtons have grown from new-age oyster farmers into restaurateurs, while helping Bay oysters rebound.

They've built oyster houses in Virginia and DC, and their most recent gift to bivalve lovers is BRINE. Its atmosphere is youthful and energetic, reflecting a triumph over gluttony and misfortune — and projecting an optimism that Bay oysters have been saved for future generations. The décor is industrial chic with minimal artwork of oyster photographs mounted on the walls. A wood-burning stove and an open kitchen enhance the warm vibe. An in-house inventory of 150+ whiskeys helps move things along as well.

Launched last year, BRINE dishes up three brands of the Croxton's bivalves that carry you through a full favor pinwheel from sweet to salty: Rappahannock River oysters, Stingrays and Olde Salts (which are half price at happy hour). Other raw bar treats include Olde Salt clams, citrus-marinated fish ceviche and Carolina shrimp cocktail. Bacon-enriched Barcat oyster chowder and lambs and clams stew require country bread for scooping up the juices. Entrée standouts include sea scallops with seared Swiss char and cannellini beans and oak-grilled duck with roasted grapes. Flatiron steak and burgers accommodate meat eaters.

Sea Pearl Restaurant & Lounge

8191 Strawberry Lane
Falls Church, VA 22042
(703) 372-5161
www.seapearlrestaurant.com

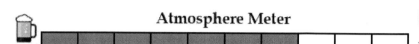

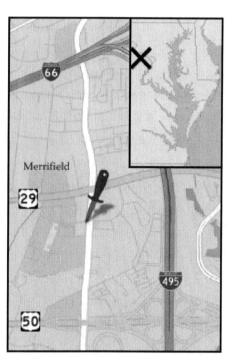

In the eight years that Sea Pearl has stood on the corner of Strawberry Lane, the neighborhood has transformed. A once-sleepy suburb, which used to be anchored by its gardening center, has now sprouted movie theaters, department stores and hip dining spots thanks to new development. It was called Merrifield, but now Mosaic District better suits the amalgamation of diverse cultures.

Since its beginning, Sea Pearl has blended Asian and American cuisines, so it fits perfectly into the renewal concept. Bivalve enthusiasts put the restaurant on their must-visit list because of the unique partnership between oysters and sushi. The menu starts with a noteworthy roll call of mainly East Coast oysters: Chincoteagues (VA), Chesapeakes (MD), Blue Points (NY), Wellfleets (MA), Malpeques (PEI) and

Kumamotos (CA). Don't leave without trying some of the "pearlized oysters" sprinkled with salmon or flying fish roe, which adds an exotic texture and savory pop to every bite. Chilled topneck clams, shrimp cocktail and spicy tuna tartare join the cool raw bar selections.

Next on the menu is top-notch sushi, which takes oysters, soft-shell crab, shrimp and other local delicacies and tucks them inside sticky rice rolls. The Far East meets the Bay's Eastern Shore in dishes such as rice cracker-encrusted crab cakes and grilled shrimp with kung pao brussel sprouts.

The décor is simply exquisite. On the outdoor patio nautical rope combined with oriental foliage underscore the restaurant's duality. Inside, guests are wowed by the gorgeous circular bar with mother-of-pearl chandeliers and dark walnut floors. Stunning curtains made with strings of capiz shells divide the dining rooms, and subtle lighting creates a sophisticated ambience. A shiny glass case atop the sushi bar lures guests to its gifts from the sea.

Northern Virginia

Trio Grill

8100 Lee Highway
Falls Church, VA 22042
(703) 992-9200
www.triomerrifield.com

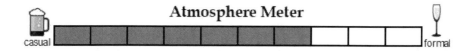

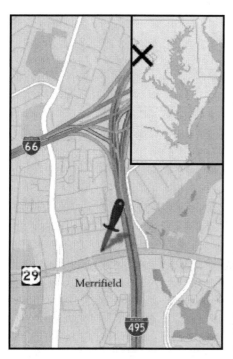

Urban elegance beyond the Beltway is what you find at Trio Grill. It's not a stuffy kind of sophistication where jackets and pressed shirts are required. Instead, this neighborhood grill wants guests to loosen their ties and unwind in comfortable contemporary surroundings.

Exposed brick, subtle lighting and a smattering of modern art (including a fantastic portrait of Marilyn Monroe) set a metropolitan motif. The lovely outdoor patio, cigar lounge and live music lighten the mood and brighten the atmosphere.

Floor-to-ceiling glass cabinets filled with wine and 50+ beers from around the world challenge you to think globally when pairing beverages with oysters. Fortunately, a variety of East Coast bivalves is at the ready with brands such as

Sweet Jesus and Chesapeake Gold from Maryland, as well as Virginia's Sewansecott and Chincoteague Salt.

Baked Chesapeake oysters topped with smoky béchamel sauce and bacon breadcrumbs kick off the seafood starters along with tempura shrimp, tuna tartare nachos and fried calamari. Fish fans dive into dishes such as porcini-crusted scallops and lobster stew with shrimp and mussels lounging in tomato fennel broth. Carnivores enjoy comfort food taken to a new level with pan-seared duck breast, braised lamb shank, grilled pork chops and juicy steaks.

Trio Grill arrived on the Northern Virginia scene in 2013 as the newest member of Metropolitan Hospitality Group, which also owns CIRCA bistro-style cafes in Clarendon and Washington, DC. Merrifield Wine & Beer, Trio's busy next-door neighbor, is also a part of this growing food and beverage team bringing fine American fare to the region.

Mussel Bar & Grille Arlington

800 North Glebe Road
Arlington, VA 22203
(703) 841-2337
www.musselbar.com

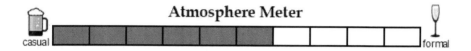

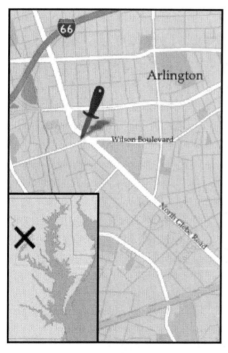

It takes a lot of muscle to hold up a 12-story building amidst the new architectural towers in Arlington's Ballston section. The mighty Mussel Bar at the base of a dazzling glass and metal structure shows its industrial strength while serving Belgian-style bivalves.

Spaces under the shadow of such a formidable edifice could have a low dark feel. Not the case with this restaurant. Its designers made the most of soaring windows and high ceilings to welcome daylight and create a bright airy vibe. Plus clever touches make the room visually engaging: chandeliers made out of beer bottles, glossy tiles on the walls and a brick patio that takes mollusks to the streets. Action from the open kitchen and shucking station catch everyone's attention.

Oyster shells embedded into tall tables around the bar give a sign that this place gets pumped up about bivalves. Its signature dish takes mussels in four delicious directions, from getting steamed in white wine with roasted garlic to smoking hot with spicy Thai green curry.

This member of the Mussel Bar trinity, along with its sister restaurants in Bethesda and Baltimore, features buck-a-shuck happy hours and hosts an annual oyster festival in the fall to showcase local aquafarms.

Raw bar choices favor oysters, clams, shrimp, lobster, or crab and seaweed salad. Dipping options include cocktail sauce, apple mignonette, Old Bay aioli, remoulade and salsa verde. Two or three local oysters are offered weekly, with Rappahannocks, Blue Points and Wild Chesapeakes from Hoopers Island on display during a recent visit. The regular menu strikes a reasonable balance between dishes from the land and the sea. Maryland crab cakes and grilled salmon peacefully coexist with burgers and smoked pork ribs. They're all tied together with a roster of 95 beers on the wall and an extensive wine list.

Lyon Hall

3100 North Washington Boulevard
Arlington, VA 22201
(703) 741-7636
www.lyonhallarlington.com

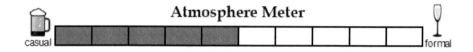

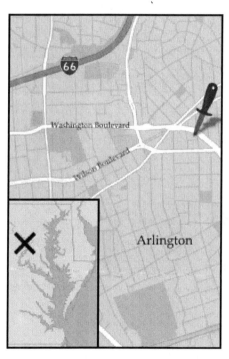

Think about a cozy corner bistro where city life parades past your table, sunlight warms your seat on the patio and oysters cool your tongue on hot summer days. In sweater weather, you move inside the bustling brasserie to leisurely sip smooth red wines and concoct credible reasons for not returning to the office.

That fanciful image is a reality at Lyon Hall. Owners of this French-inspired eatery restored a historic North Arlington art deco building, preserved its vintage character and created a charming setting for oyster aficionados. It's part of a restaurant family that includes Liberty Tavern and Northside Social in Clarendon and creates comfortable gathering places. The décor is simple yet sophisticated, and its muted gray color scheme gracefully contrasts with black and dark wood furniture.

Tables are crowded with fresh-baked baguettes, house-cured charcuterie meats and hand-crafted cheeses, all of which are locally sourced. Usually two or three Chesapeake oysters make the list, and the chef rotates regional brands to give regular guests a variety of tastes. During a recent visit, Chesapeake Golds (MD) and Moonstones (RI) arrived on a silver tray with ice. Shrimp cocktail and tuna tartare are perfect chilled companions.

Mussels are steamed four different ways, including an exceptional dish cooked with bratwurst, leeks and gruyere cheese in a Dijon white wine broth. Seafood bouillabaisse tumbles seafood treasures in a saffron tomato sauce that requires extra bread for soaking up every drop. The rest of the menu plays like a favorite song of French and German classics: warm Bavarian pretzels, pork jägerschnitzel, Bohemian sausage platter and more. All of this, with 23 beers on tap and 50 in bottles, are good reasons to come here often.

Clyde's at Mark Center

1700 North Beauregard Street
Alexandria, VA 22311
(703) 820-8300
www.clydes.com/mark-center

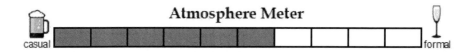

Atmosphere Meter

casual — formal

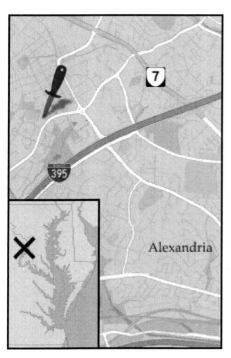

Plenty of places offer oyster lists and shuckers, but only Clyde's prints an Oyster Eater's Bill of Rights on the raw bar menu. It's a bold declaration that oysters here are laboratory tested, harvested in season from clean waters, named on the menu by species and location, received from certified shellfish shippers, and expertly shucked and presented on ice within five minutes of opening.

It's also your personal guarantee that bivalves are served by knowledgeable staff who can suggest pairings of oyster-friendly wines and ales. Every day, fresh oysters are delivered to the kitchen and posted for your selection. Kusshi (BC), Pemaquid and Weskeag (ME), Sunberry Point (PEI), Navy Point (NY), Salt Pond (RI), and Wellfleet (MA) were on the list during a recent visit. Other members of the raw bar

Northern Virginia **219**

crew include littleneck clams, shrimp, crab claws and lobster cocktail. They're all half price during oyster hour.

The regular menu is a deluge of seafood that features Chesapeake staples such as jumbo lump crab cakes, grilled rockfish and flash-fried cod fish and chips. Chicken, pork, steaks and burgers are prepared for meat eaters.

Clyde's at Mark Center not only serves oysters to match any taste, but the 350-seat restaurant houses dining rooms to fit any mood, especially if you're fond of sporting life on the water. The Crew Bar looks like an old Potomac boathouse with pictures of rowing regattas and oyster-harvesting skipjacks. The Adirondack Room feels like a rustic fishing camp, featuring a stone fireplace, Indian blanket upholstery, and moose and deer heads. The Chesapeake Room resembles an Eastern Shore hunt club, and its fireplace is flanked by gun racks and antique duck decoys. The Newport Room, decked out like a yacht, celebrates boats of America's Cup races. It's all a magical maze that toasts oysters and fun on the waves.

Legal Sea Foods Restaurant & Oyster Bar Arlington – Crystal City

2301 Jefferson Davis Highway
Arlington, VA 22202
(703) 415-1200
www.legalseafoods.com

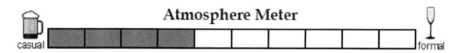

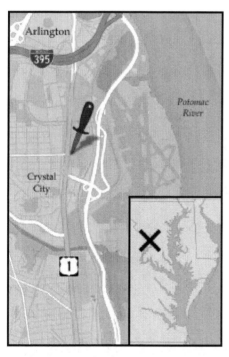

This branch of Legal Seafood is located just off Jefferson Davis Highway next to Crystal City's huge retail center that is an underground complex of more than 100 stores and services. When you come to this neighborhood, consider taking the "Shop & Shuck Challenge." The goal is to buy all your holiday gifts and gadgets in record time, so you can leisurely indulge in cocktails and munchies.

Legal Sea Foods' long dining room has lots of space to stash shopping bags, and the bartender shakes soothing drinks guaranteed to help you recuperate from the gift-gathering blitzkrieg. Hot-buttered rum or the

Espresso Martini with Kahlúa, Baileys Irish Cream and vodka, should do the trick nicely. The extensive dessert menu is an added bonus for comforting weary shoppers.

Legal Sea Foods, a Massachusetts-based company, is taking the East Coast by storm from Rhode Island to Georgia by offering fresh fish and farmed oysters from the Atlantic seaboard. During a recent Shop & Shuck day, the list offered northern bivalves including Wellfleet, Merry, Sandy Neck and Wianno oysters from Massachusetts, and Kusshi out of British Columbia. Oysters baked with spinach, cheese, herb crumbs and morsels of lobster are terrific, and fried oysters, BBQ and Buffalo-style, give a good crunch.

New England fried clams and shrimp cocktail kick off the regular menu's appetizers, followed by seafood standouts such as the Portuguese Fisherman's Stew and a classic lobster bake loaded with littleneck clams, mussels, chorizo and corn. Steaks, BBQ ribs and vegetarian dishes make everyone happy.

McCormick & Schmick's Arlington

2010 Crystal Drive
Arlington, VA 22202
(703) 413-6400
www.mccormickandschmicks.com

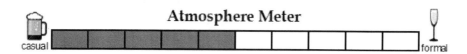

Atmosphere Meter

casual — formal

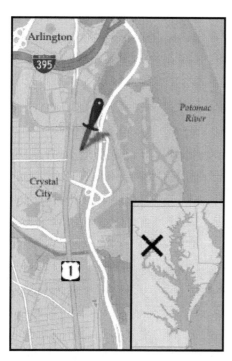

McCormick & Schmick's Crystal City franchise near National Airport is a convenient home base for DC visitors and bivalve seekers. Quicker than you'd expect from a Virginia address, you can get to Arlington Cemetery, National Harbor, Old Town Alexandria, the National Mall and other popular sites.

Located near the Potomac River not far from where George Washington gathered bivalves for his family's dinner centuries ago, it's a fine spot for sampling oysters that are grown and harvested with today's new aquafarming techniques. During a recent visit, East Coast boutique oysters were the headliners:

Maryland's Skinny Dippers and Choptank Sweets, Virginia's James Rivers, and Connecticut's Blue Points.

Oysters Rockefeller are bubbling bites of bivalves topped with spinach, Pernod and hollandaise. Steamed mussels swim in a savory pool of white wine, tomatoes and herbs. Other noteworthy seafood starters include spicy seared tuna, crispy fried calamari and bacon-wrapped shrimp dusted with pepper jack cheese. Entrees read like an Atlantic fisherman's guide featuring salmon, striped bass, rainbow trout and flounder. They're made any way you like — grilled, broiled or pan-seared. Steaks, burgers and chicken are also available.

McCormick & Schmick's passion for aquatic edibles carries over into the décor, with wooden fish and pictures of oyster shells, crabs and crayfish hanging on the walls. Privacy booths with sleek golden swags encourage intimate dining. Bold 1960s retro light fixtures and mod fabrics on the chairs give this location a more casual vibe than some of its upscale M&S sister restaurants that sport a Victorian saloon theme.

Northern Virginia

Hank's Oyster Bar Old Town

1026 King Street
Alexandria, VA 22314
(703) 739-4265
www.hanksoysterbar.com

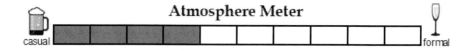

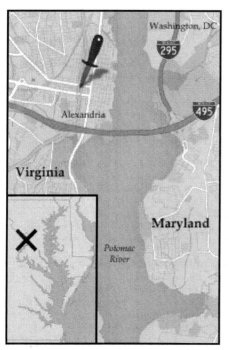

Founded in 1749, Old Town Alexandria hosts more than 20 historic sites from colonial times to the Civil War. Antique shops, chic boutiques, art galleries and lively pubs line the quaint cobblestone streets.

Hank's Oyster Bar is located on one of the main avenues, but far enough away from the waterfront to avoid the Potomac's annual flooding and the torrents of pedestrian traffic.

The restaurant is easy for oyster seekers to find. Look for a double-wide rowhouse painted a cheerful ocean blue. In the front windows you'll see customers scooping forks into trays of Chesapeake oysters. At the shucking station near the back of the bar, bivalves are laid out in icy bins with signs marking their brands. Sweet Jesus and Chesapeake Gold from Maryland, White Stone and

Salty Wolfe from Virginia; and Arcadia, Pickering Pass and Eld Inlet from Washington State were nestled in cool compartments during a recent visit.

This newest edition to the Hank's family has the same upbeat welcoming atmosphere as its sister restaurants in Dupont Circle and Capital Hill. And they're all packed with award-winning fresh seafood.

Sake oyster shooters, shrimp cocktail and fish ceviche team up with oysters at the ice bar. Small plates that feature local bivalves include fried oysters, garlic steamed Blue Bay mussels and oysters Rockefeller with bacon. Middleneck clams are steamed in tomato and white wine butter sauce. Crab cakes and lobster rolls with Old Bay fries show the chef's affinity for East Coast beach fare classics.

Meat eaters never feel left out at Hank's, thanks to dishes such as lamb and bleu cheese burgers, grilled duck breast, braised short ribs and crispy Southern fried chicken. Craft cocktails change with the season. Autumn specials include Dark & Stormy (rum, ginger beer and lime juice) and Fall Fling (Jim Beam rye, amaretto, apple cider and lemon).

Columbia Firehouse Restaurant & Barroom

109 South St. Asaph Street
Alexandria, VA 22314
(703) 683-1776
www.columbiafirehouse.com

Atmosphere Meter

casual |▓|▓|▓|▓|▓|▓|▓| | | | formal

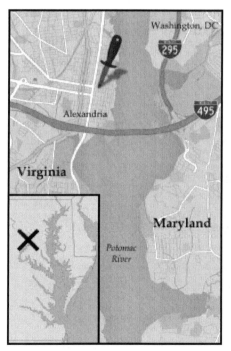

Columbia Firehouse offers a unique opportunity to dine on oysters while stepping back in time and imagining life during the Chesapeake Bay's 19th century seafood heyday.

In 1871, Alexandria initiated the Columbia Steam Engine Fire Company, and this building was its home. Nearly 144 years later, this historic structure was restored giving Old Town an exquisite piece of its past.

The exterior looks almost the same as when it was built with beautiful red brickwork and graceful arched windows. The interior preservation is spectacular. Each of the four levels showcases stunning stained glass laid into dark mahogany woodwork. The atrium's tall glass ceiling creates a playful rivalry between the light fixtures' sparkling candles and the twinkling stars above. The atmosphere is elegant and magical. The wrought iron spiral staircase conjures up images of firefighters rushing to save the town from flames.

Oysters on the half shell arrive stylishly dressed for the occasion with crimson cocktail sauce and cucumber sriracha mignonette. During a recent visit, Holy Grail, HongaTonk and Assateague Wild Ponies oysters made the A-list for the evening. Littleneck clams and shrimp cocktail are their escorts at the raw bar. Mussels are steamed three different ways: in white wine with tomatoes and garlic, curry and coconut milk, and pilsner with bacon and cream.

The rest of the menu skillfully balances seafood with meat dishes. Calamari, tuna tartare and plump crab cakes showcase ingredients from the ocean, while steaks, lamb, pork shanks and grilled half chicken accommodate landlubbers' pleasures. Collard greens and brussel sprouts add a dash of healthy greens on the side.

Overwood

220 North Lee Street
Alexandria, VA 22314
(703) 535-3340
www.theoverwood.com

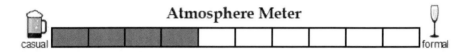

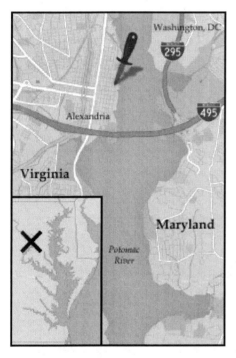

Overwood might be one of the few places in town that buys cords of wood in the summer from a local farmer. That's because the kitchen staff prepares food the old-fashioned way — in wood-burning ovens. The reward for their efforts is smoky rich flavors in food and alluring aromas that drift down the street.

The restaurant is located in an historic building just off the main drag and a short stroll away from the waterfront. The warm cozy atmosphere creates a relaxed setting for dining on fresh shucked oysters. Chincoteagues and Wiannos were featured during a recent visit. The full list of bivalves that are rotated on a regular basis reads like an oyster lover's tour of paradise: Wellfleet, Malpeque, Beau Soleil, Blue Point, James River, Rappahannock, Misty Point, Watch House, Choptank Sweet,

Sewansecott, Sweet Jesus and Salt Grass Point. PEI mussels steamed in white wine and lemon broth are heavenly.

When you scan the menu, let the wood-burning oven's aroma guide your selections. Seafood standouts include scallops with basmati rice, Atlantic salmon with oven-roasted garlic mashed potatoes and a big bowl of shrimp jambalaya with andouille sausage and chicken breast in a tomato Cajun broth. Meat eaters cherish signature dishes such as Blackstrap molasses and rum baby back ribs, wood-grilled porterhouse pork chops and Black Angus New York strip steaks.

The soothing décor, centered on exposed brick walls, muted earth tones and framed black-and-white photos, encourages diners to linger longer and enjoy house special desserts. Top picks: fudge brownie sundae and Elvis Pie with banana, peanut butter, chocolate and whipped cream baked inside an Oreo cookie crust that's too good for sharing.

Blackwall Hitch Alexandria

5 Cameron Street
Alexandria, VA 22314
(571) 982-3577
www.theblackwallhitch.com

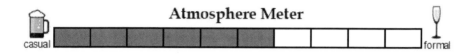

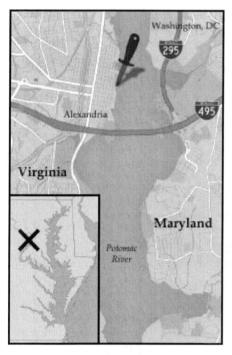

Blackwall Hitch made quite a splash when it came to the Old Town waterfront last year. It landed a prime location between the Potomac River and Torpedo Factory Art Center where an endless stream of visitors enjoy activities and exhibits at the lively port.

The building was once a ho-hum food court, but designers converted the space into an oyster-eating utopia. The massive black metal and glass structure hosts two outdoor patios with marvelous riverside views and fire pits to deflect cool breezes from the water. The black metal design theme continues inside and is softened by candles, flowers and light blue glassware on rustic wooden tables. In a loft space above the dining room is The Crow's Nest, a laid-back lounge area decked out with overstuffed sofas and comfy chairs.

Cocktails are mixed at four different bars, but one holds particular interest to bivalve hunters — the oyster bar. On its cool white marble top awaits an array of brands from the Chesapeake Bay and beyond. Chincoteagues, Choptank Sweets, Blue Points and Malpeques were placed on icy trays during a recent visit. Baked oysters are topped with inventive ingredients from savory bacon to toasted coconut and petite crab cakes.

The menu is similar to its sister restaurant in Annapolis, offering seafood harvested from the region's waters. Steamed clams and mussels are accompanied by warm artisan bread, and Maryland crab soup simmers in traditional tomato broth. Chesapeake steamers boil crab, shrimp, scallops, mussels and clams in a seafood stock with corn, kielbasa and potatoes. Steaks, sandwiches, lamb chops and an Eastern Shore chicken pot pie deliver dining options for meat lovers.

Fish Market Restaurant & Raw Bar

105 King Street
Alexandria, VA 22314
(703) 836-5676
www.fishmarketva.com

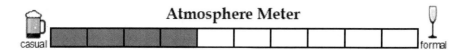

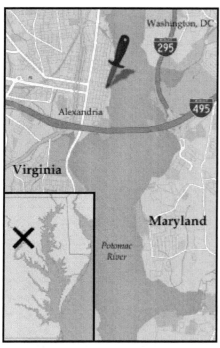

At the Fish Market your oyster adventure begins at the front window display case, where only a sheet of glass comes between you and a cornucopia of seafood.

Among the lobsters, fish, snow crab legs and clams blanketed in ice are oysters bearing little signs that herald many of the Bay's best bivalves. Regular guests in this seafood bounty include Tom's Cove, Tarkill Creek, Cannon Cove, Sea Rexx and Hoopers Island oysters.

Inside the restaurant, a shucker stands at his station popping open bushels of bivalves for half-shell presentations, while kitchen staff adds some heat to the mix of mollusks. Bowls are filled with creamy New England clam chowder, and fried oysters come with remoulade sauce on a toasted bun. Peel and eat shrimp are doused in Old Bay spices. The menu's nautical theme highlights Fish Market's commitment to fresh local catch. Crab cakes, grilled sea scallops and blackened rockfish are an embodiment of Chesapeake cuisine. Landlubbers aren't left high and dry with options such as steaks, burgers and char-grilled chicken platters.

The sprawling restaurant is home to five dining rooms and 400 seats. The décor varies from The Anchor Bar with 16 HD TVs to calm spaces with exposed brick walls, colorful murals and photos of Chesapeake watermen. A patio and balcony appeal to alfresco fans in warm weather.

On a wall upstairs, you can read the life story of this historic building. More than 200 years old, it originally stored ships' cargo from around the world. During the Civil War, it morphed into a hospital for Confederate troops, and a bold tenant brewed beer for thirsty Virginians during Prohibition. With 40 ales on tap at the bar, the Fish Market does its best to uphold such honorable traditions.

Union Street Public House

121 South Union Street
Alexandria, VA 22314
(703) 548-1785
www.unionstreetpublichouse.com

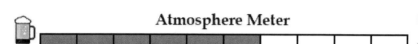
Atmosphere Meter
casual — formal

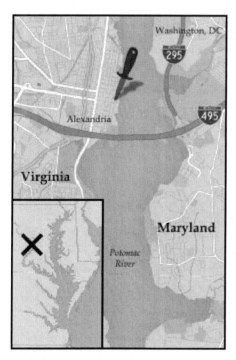

Union Street's beautiful brown brick building has graced Alexandria's waterfront since 1785. Originally erected as a mercantile warehouse for storing dry goods and other sundries, it became a popular gathering place for citizens, businessmen and seafaring ship captains.

Documents show that George Washington often left his nearby Mount Vernon home to meet with town leaders and fellow rebel rousers inside these walls. Upstairs, a special room commemorates this famous patron with paintings of the first U.S. president. Local lore says that the ghost of a young girl appears in the Washington Room, searching for something. Perhaps she is looking for oysters. If that's the case, then she has come to the right place.

The apparition should float downstairs and follow a sign for the oyster bar, where skilled shuckers prepare icy trays without a fleck of sand or speck of shell — just plump oysters reclining in their pristine juices. Usually two or three brands make the daily list, namely Blue Points (NY) and White Stones (VA) on a recent visit. Don't leave without tasting the house specialty Wally's Oysters baked with bacon and chive butter.

Fried oysters and smoked oyster chowder spearhead the menu along with shrimp beignets and creamy scallops Rockefeller. Other outstanding ocean treats include steamed mussels, robust crab cakes, grilled salmon BLT and blackened red snapper. Noteworthy meat dishes: fried chicken and waffles, thick-cut steaks and juicy pork loin. In addition to fine food, Union Street has a cheerful, neighborhood tavern vibe and a staff that greets guests like old friends. Add in lovely décor accented by a subtle boating theme, and you'll find yourself returning here for oysters as often as you can.

236 Virginia Peninsulas

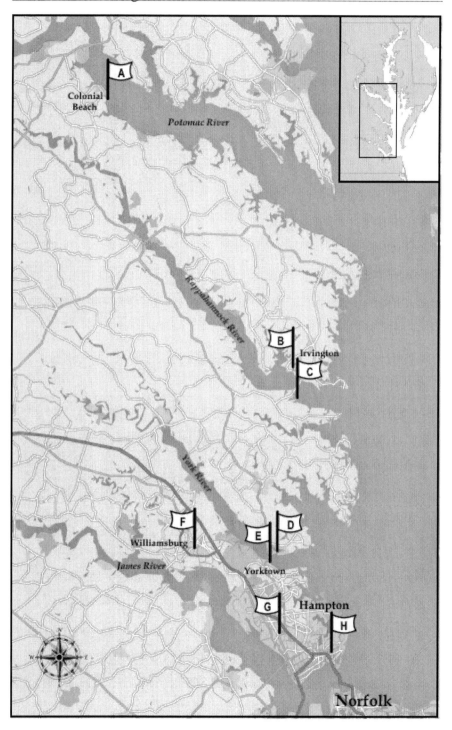

Virginia Peninsulas

- Ⓐ Denson's Grocery & R&B Oyster Bar 238
- Ⓑ Tides Inn 240
- Ⓒ Merroir 242
- Ⓓ York River Oyster Company 244
- Ⓔ Yorktown Pub 246
- Ⓕ Berret's Seafood Restaurant & Taphouse Grill 248
- Ⓖ Harpoon Larry's Fish House & Oyster Bar 250
- Ⓗ Crabtown Raw Bar & Grille 252

Virginia Peninsulas

Denson's Grocery & R&B Oyster Bar

117 Washington Avenue
Colonial Beach, VA 22443
(804) 224-4121
www.densonsgrocery.com

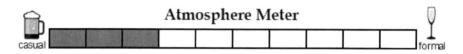

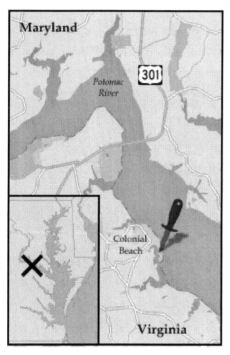

Most country stores are stocked with bait, fishing tackle and canned goods, but the shelves at Denson's are a foodie's delight, harboring everything from Spanish olives to gourmet Southern grits. The refrigerated cases hold Boar's Head meat, fresh fish, craft beer and wine.

You can order take-out, but meals here are such a delightful experience that the screened-in patio is a much better bet. With a smile that lights up the room, the owner welcomes guests as if they are old chums. Three generations of this family-owned business are the epitome of Southern hospitality. Plus, they love oysters. They are passionate about local and East Coast bivalves, so you're likely to find them offering brands such as

Madhouse, Black Horse, Sewansecott, Rappahannock, Wellfleet or Tauton Bay with a divine watermelon mignonette that perfectly balances sweet with briny flavors.

House special roasted oysters Drago Style, Rockefeller and Cackalacky are savory one-bite wonders. Fried oysters carry a flawless crunch, and Northern Neck oyster stew is a silky bowl of bivalves, butter, cream and seasonings. Crab cakes, grilled rockfish, bluefish dip and steamed mussels showcase Chesapeake Bay classics. Porterhouse steaks and thick sandwiches keep meat eaters coming back for more.

This quaint eatery resides in Colonial Beach, a seaside town on the Potomac. It played a role in a period of Bay history called the Oyster Wars that rivaled the mayhem of the Wild West. In the mid-1900s, over-harvesting reduced the oyster beds to such a level that violence and gunshots erupted between watermen from Maryland and Virginia. This area was a haven for the Mosquito Fleet, a band of locals who unlawfully dredged oysters and used high-speed boats to evade police and escape into the safety of Monroe Bay.

Virginia Peninsulas

Tides Inn

480 King Carter Drive
Irvington, VA 22480
(804) 438-4489
www.tidesinn.com

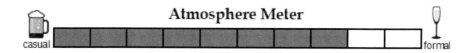

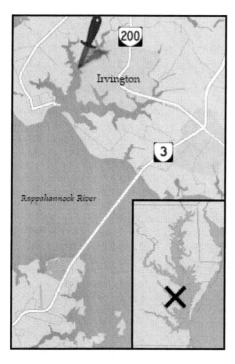

For thousands of years, people around the world have whispered that oysters are a potent and exotic food. Ancient Romans' belief in their aphrodisiac powers put oysters on the table for grand dinners and naughty orgies. It's rumored that the Roman emperor Vitellius downed nearly 1,000 bivalves at such a lusty event to get his juices flowing. Casanova, the 18th century ladies man, nibbled 50 oysters a day during his morning bath so he could rise to the occasion for his 122 willing women.

So, is it a coincidence that Tides Inn is one of the most romantic getaways on the Bay, and it serves an abundance of oysters? Perhaps not. Amore is certainly in the air at this luxury resort nestled in a beautiful bivalve stronghold along Carters Creek and the Rappahannock River. Oysters farmed in the nearby creek are brought to the kitchen daily and treated like celebrity guests by the chef. The award-winning house specialty, Angry Oysters, is prepared Buffalo style with hot and sour cabbage, watermelon rind salsa and pickled radish. You can get a dozen on the half shell with a bubbling flute of prosecco, crispy fried on a platter, or roasted with parmesan butter and gremolada.

Other regional dishes include broiled rockfish, Old Bay steamed shrimp, panko-crusted flounder, Chesapeake crab cakes and Seafood Bolognese with mussels, shrimp and scallops in an herbed butter over fettuccini. Steaks, chicken and pasta are on the menu, but seafood steals the show here.

If you want to get up close and personal with the area's oysters, Tides Inn arranges excursions with watermen to show how bivalves are grown and harvested at local aquafarms. The chef offers special sessions on roasting oysters and reveals cooking tips you can bring home to your kitchen. After these activities are over, you can relax at the evening firepits and unleash the romantic magic of Chesapeake oysters.

Merroir

784 Locklies Creek Road
Topping, VA 23169
(804) 758-2871
www.rroysters.com

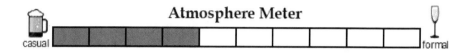

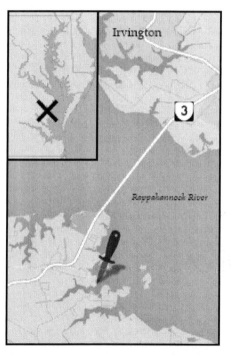

Merroir is located in Topping, VA (pop. 1,165), a quaint rural outpost on the Middle Peninsula of the Bay. The restaurant resides in a plain white building with picnic tables spread out along the water under the shade of a few umbrellas and a big old tree. The stunning view reveals a sleepy marina, mounds of oyster shells and serene waterfront.

Merroir's beauty lies in its simplicity: fresh local ingredients prepared on an outdoor grill by a seafood-savvy chef. Three types of oysters, which are designed to satisfy your taste buds' entire flavor wheel, are served here: Rappahannocks (sweet), Stingrays (mild) and Old Salts (briny). You can savor them raw on the half shell or let the chef display his finesse with Bay bivalves in dishes such as oysters roasted in garlic butter, Angels on Horseback baked with herbed butter and Edwards ham, and BBQ bourbon chipotle grilled oysters. Sample as many as you like but do not leave this place without tasting the incredible Stuffin' Muffin, a delectable grilled patty of oyster stuffing and bacon covered with peppercorn cream. The menu changes with the season's harvests, but you can always count on fresh seafood. Among the favorites are Bay scallops ceviche with tortilla chips, skate wing with lemon and caper butter sauce, and steamed Carolina shrimp. Lamb and clam stew is a spicy union of the land and sea in a bowl.

But there's more than meets the eye to this hidden gem's fine food and pastoral setting. In the waters beyond your table is an aquafarm that's a powerhouse in resurrecting Chesapeake oysters. It's home to the famous Rappahannock Oyster Co., owned by the Croxton family since 1899 and operated by two cousins whose mission to help Bay oysters flourish is unflinching. Their oysters are devoured across America and are regarded as some of the world's finest.

Virginia Peninsulas

York River Oyster Company

8109 Yacht Haven Road
Gloucester Point, VA 23062
(804) 993-7174
www.yorkriveroysterco.com

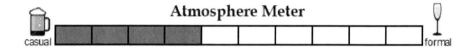

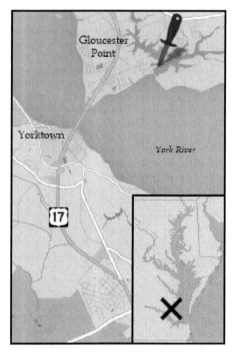

When York River Oyster Company promises that you'll have a shell of a good time at its restaurant, it's not kidding around. It's located at a delightful spot along the river where you can wile away hours watching the waterfront fun. Live music on weekends, usually acoustic guitar, brightens the mood. Whether you come by car or boat, the marina store ensures you have all the supplies you need for a fantastic day at the Bay.

An outside dock bar creates a casual setting for cold beer on hot summer days. Two inside dining rooms are separated by a large open window frame and decorated with subtle nautical artwork. A large blue and red crab made out of an old muffler hangs above the door, signaling that fresh and artfully presented seafood awaits.

The York River is renowned for producing some of the best oysters in the Chesapeake watershed, and all of the ones served here are harvested locally. On a recent trip, Charlie Rock Rappahannocks, Big Island Guineas and Baypoint York River oysters appeared on the plate, orchestrating an ideal buttery-to-briny medley of flavors. The raw bar covers the essentials with an array of chilled choices: peel n' eat shrimp, clams, mussels and snow crab legs. Hungry customers have consumed so many oysters here that the restaurant recently donated 132 bushels of shells to the Chesapeake Bay Foundation for reef preservation efforts.

The menu is flush with other seafood options. Oysters Rockefeller, crispy calamari and crab dip with Old Bay corn chips lead the appetizer pack. Fried oysters, blackened fish tacos, shrimp scampi and Dickey's seafood paella rank among the favorite entrées. If you happen to stop by for Sunday brunch, you will feel blessed while eating the crab cake on sweet corn bread with spinach and roasted red pepper hollandaise sauce. Burgers, pork and chicken are also on tap.

Virginia Peninsulas

Yorktown Pub

540 Water Street
Yorktown, VA 23690
(757) 886-9964
www.yorktownpub.com

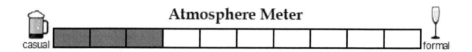

Yorktown Pub is located just a brief stroll from the battlefield where George Washington and his French allies forced England's Cornwallis to surrender in 1781 and conclude the American Revolution.

The building was erected in 1951, and this homey tavern's interior has knotty pine walls, booths with green leather seats, a long wooden bar with a brass railing and nautical items as wall décor. A soothing smoky aroma rises from the wood-burning fireplace. It's the type of bar where you feel welcomed instantly, and the atmosphere is friendly and laid-back.

Its waterfront location along the York River beach makes it easy for local watermen to deliver oysters daily, and most of the seafood is pulled out of the Poquoson and York Rivers and other spots around the Gloucester area. The staff gladly tells background stories about the oysters served, so you're certain to take away an insider's view of the regional seafood.

Fresh shucked York River oysters and middleneck clams (steamed or raw on the half shell) jumpstart the appetizers, along with spiced jumbo shrimp and fried fish mini tacos. The "Oh Gee" Oyster Stack builds a tasty tower of grilled ham, pepporcini, tomatoes and oysters.

Other seafood specialties include the pub's famous grilled lump crab cakes, Cape May sea scallops, fried oyster platter, Maine lobster roll and Big Island ahi tuna from the Outer Banks of North Carolina. From the land, you find Boar's Head deli meat sandwiches, Jamaican jerk chicken, vinegar-based Carolina BBQ and smoking hot chili. Local micro beers are featured in weekly specials as the perfect companion for buck-a-shuck oysters and clams.

Virginia Peninsulas

Berret's Seafood Restaurant & Taphouse Grill

199 South Boundary Street
Williamsburg, VA 23185
(757) 253-1847
www.berrets.com

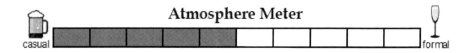

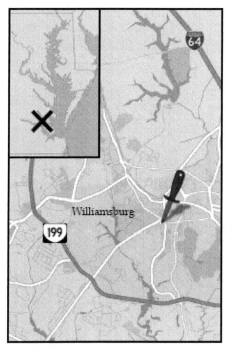

Stationed between the College of William & Mary and crowds of tourists hoping to relive the Colonial America experience in Williamsburg is an oyster eaters' haven called Berret's. The main restaurant is rather large with several dining rooms, but stain glass partitions carve out privacy seating that makes the place feel less cavernous. It's a nice sit-down kind of tavern that showcases local artwork.

The Taphouse and outdoor patio sport a more casual vibe, hosting live bands and "Steal the Pint" evenings that explore local craft beers. In both sections, oysters play a key role on the menu. Bargain hunters can slurp $1 Happy Hour oysters without putting a dent in their wallets. Tommy

Leggett's York River oysters and James River oysters are house staples, and on a recent visit Shooting Point Nassawadox oysters were on the chalkboard. Oysters Rockefeller, traditional oyster stew and Berret's baked oysters with crab meat, ham and bread crumbs are delicious. Flash-fried oysters come with remoulade sauce for dipping.

An herb garden in the front yard is a reassuring sign that the kitchen cares about freshness. Seafood comes from local waters in tasty dishes such as steamed mussels, lump crab cakes and bacon-wrapped whole rainbow trout. Regional meat plates include rib eyes, chicken and braised short ribs.

As you stroll around the cobblestone streets, consider the idea that oysters likely changed the course of history for our early colonists. Bivalves grew in such abundance here that Algonquin Indians named the waters "Chesepiook," meaning "great shellfish bay." In 1609, a brutal winter hit Jamestown settlement, and only 60 of the original 214 pioneers lived. The fortunate ones survived by eating oysters and shellfish.

Harpoon Larry's Fish House & Oyster Bar

621 J. Clyde Morris Boulevard
Newport News, VA 23601
(757) 827-0600
www.harpoonlarrys.com

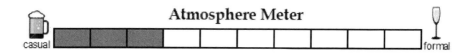

Atmosphere Meter

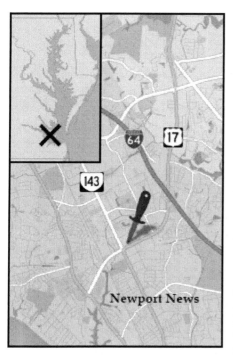

The second you walk through the door at Harpoon Larry's you sense that you're in for a special oyster-eating experience. A large metal cage filled to the top with oyster shells behind the hostess stand is your first clue. Then you spy on the wall the extensive oyster list, and you know you've arrived at Oysterpalooza.

Above the shucking station and underneath a massive mounted shark hangs a chalkboard with an impressive array of local bivalves. From Virginia: Captain Jax, Hog Islands, Seaside Salts, Ships Points, Mobjack Bays, Windmill Points, Chincoteagues, Shooting Points, Pocahontas, Seaford Stars and Bay Points.

Beside the litany of the Old Dominion's best bivalves is a lengthy roster of northeast oysters — Blue Points (CT), Wellfleets (MA) and Malpeques (PEI) — to name a few. As if that wasn't enough, the menu thoughtfully describes each oyster's flavor from mild to salty so you can choose brands to suit your taste. So, go ahead and take an East Coast oyster tour. The prices are reasonable, and the shucker is agreeable.

The atmosphere is energetic, almost festive. Large trophy fish are nailed to the walls along with photos of proud sports fishermen displaying their prize catch. Wood booths line up below the windows, and a screened patio waits outside.

Seafood is the menu's centerpiece with oysters Rockefeller and Buffalo oysters leading the appetizers. Flounder, red snapper and mahi mahi are among the daily specials, and regular dishes such as shrimp and grits and fried soft-shell crabs show their southern Chesapeake roots. Local beers and fruity crushes are pleased to quench your thirst.

Crabtown Raw Bar & Grille

1405 East Pembroke Avenue
Hampton, VA 23663
(757) 723-3400
www.crabtownva.com

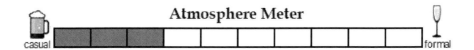

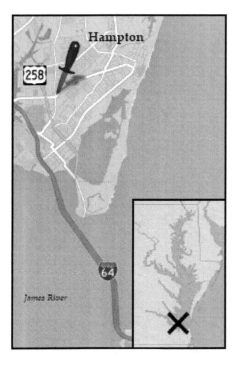

Crabtown's substantial raw bar should bring a smile to your face. Rappahannock, James River, Seaside Salt, Blue Point and Chesapeake Bay oysters from Tangier Sound wait for you to take a tiny fork, tug them from their shells and pop them into your mouth.

If the steamed shrimp, clams and snow crab legs don't elicit a grin, then the Crabtown Boil Steamer Pot with all this seafood plus potatoes, corn and andouille sausage will delight you.

The rest of the menu follows suit by presenting fresh catch from the region. Oysters appear fried in po' boy sandwiches or char-grilled in a white wine, garlic and parmesan sauce. Ahi tuna swims to the table with wasabi mayo, fish tacos are served with refried beans and corn and black bean salsa, and clams in a spicy tomato sauce rest on a bed of pasta. Steaks, meatloaf, burgers, chicken, reubens and pulled pork BBQ are on call for those who prefer meat.

The logo — a feisty crab in a martini glass holding two green olives in his claw — says the cooks don't mess around with food or drink. It's a comfy casual place that's open for breakfast, lunch and dinner.

On the dining room walls hang vintage photos of an old amusement park that used to entertain local residents. The story goes back to after the Civil War when Hampton was trying to recover from the destruction of combat. Rebuilding centered on the abundant supply of oysters and crabs in the area, and before long seafood processing plants and shucking houses dotted the shoreline. Hampton soon earned the nickname "Crabtown." In 1897, a businessman lengthened the electric trolley line to nearby Buckroe Beach and built an amusement park. During segregation, a rival park was created next door for African Americans. Unfortunately the parks fell into decline when Busch Gardens Williamsburg opened, and the parks were torn down in 1991. Hurricane Isabel demolished the fishing pier, but the city rebuilt it in 2009. Today, a beach, pavilion and recreation area are worth a visit and only a short drive from this bustling oyster and seafood house.

254 Virginia Beach & Norfolk

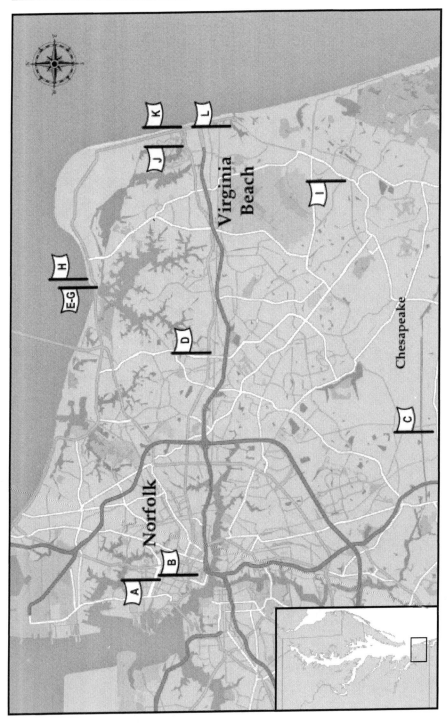

Virginia Beach & Norfolk

Virginia Beach & Norfolk

- Ⓐ A.W. Shuck's Raw Bar & Grill 256
- Ⓑ Big Easy Oyster Bar 258
- Ⓒ Bad Habits Wing & Oyster Bar 260
- Ⓓ McCormick & Schmick's Virginia Beach 262
- Ⓔ Bubba's Seafood Restaurant & Crabhouse 264
- Ⓕ Dockside Restaurant 266
- Ⓖ Chick's Oyster Bar 268
- Ⓗ Lynnhaven Fish House Restaurant 270
- Ⓘ Lucky Oyster Seafood Grill 272
- Ⓙ Metropolitan Oyster Exchange 274
- Ⓚ Catch 31 Fish House & Bar 276
- Ⓛ Rudee's Restaurant & Cabana Bar 278

A.W. Shuck's Raw Bar & Grill

2200 Colonial Avenue
Norfolk, VA 23517
(757) 664-9117

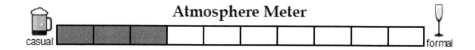

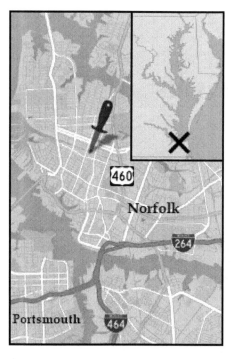

Your first glance of A.W. Shucks says that you're going to enjoy a sweet slice of vintage Norfolk. The building, a livery stable and bowling alley in previous lives, is made of rich red bricks kilned in the 1800s. Its masonry survived the Burning of Norfolk, Yellow Fever epidemic, Civil War, segregation disputes, and urban renewal of this vibrant shipping and naval town.

Today's seafood lovers are beneficiaries of the building's longevity. Tall blue murals of ferocious predatory fish on the walls near the outdoor patio set the stage for a colorful dining experience. Wooden tiki masks keep guests company in the waiting area. The dining room's casual décor features exposed brick walls, contemporary and aquatic artwork, and blonde wood furniture. The atmosphere is funky, lively and welcoming.

Virginia and East Coast oysters play leading roles on the daily special chalkboard that covers the entire back wall of the dining area. The restaurant offers a nice selection, and oyster brands rotate seasonally. On a recent visit, Pleasure Houses, Carpe Diems, Blue Points, Freeland Creeks, Sewansecotts and Malpeques were opened at the bar by an amiable and knowledgeable shucker, who admitted that the restaurant often goes through 2,000+ oysters in a week.

Oyster come on the half shell, as well as steamed and fried if you prefer them cooked. Fresh catch-of-the-day depends on the season, but usually three or four options are on tap such as catfish, flounder, shrimp, crab cakes and clams. Combo platters simplify decision making, and the kitchen aims to please every palate by offering to cook it your way – fried, broiled, blackened, or grilled. The well-rounded menu also presents options for meat eaters: chicken, steaks, burgers, and pork chops. Salads are freshly tossed, and the mac and cheese is perfect comfort food.

Virginia Beach & Norfolk

Big Easy Oyster Bar

111 West Tazewell Street
Norfolk, VA 23510
(757) 227-6222
www.bigeasygrillandoysterbar.com

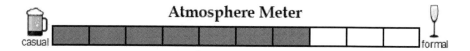

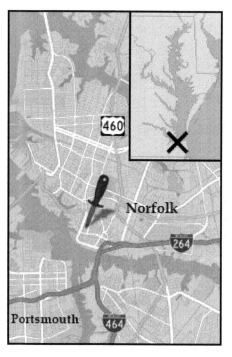

Within easy walking distance from the waterfront in a charming part of downtown Norfolk is a double-decker retreat for Chesapeake oyster fans. Big Easy Oyster Bar is on the ground level, and Norfolk Seafood Company is located on the floor above. The duo of destinations promises to satisfy your seafood desires.

The décor is lovely. Exposed brick walls and smooth wooden floors are softened with graceful curved lines. Colorful nautical flags and vintage photos of the waterfront adorn the walls, while a mermaid beckons from above the fireplace.

The raw bar is an abundant pool of Chesapeake bivalves. On a recent visit, James River, Misty Point and Seaside oysters were the stars of the show. The Large Oyster Sampler gives the chef free reign to choose 18 special mollusks pulled from Chesapeake and Atlantic waters, and the Raw Bar Platter delivers three oysters, clams, shrimp and crab salad. Fried oyster po' boys and oysters Rockefeller are delish. In keeping with its name, Big Easy offers a range of Gulf Coast treats including New Orleans shrimp and crab etouffee, gumbo and seafood jambalaya. Be sure to order Tuna Poke when it's on the list. The sushi-grade fish tossed with eel sauce and pineapple over seaweed salad is unforgettable.

When you sit at the bar slurping oysters and sipping cocktails, raise a glass to Rev. Billy Sunday. If he'd had his way in 1920, you'd be drinking water not booze. Sunday was a local preacher and Prohibition activist when Virginia went dry in 1916 — four years before the rest of America. Norfolk tried to stay wet, but the state legislature overruled the vote. When the 18th Amendment was enacted nationwide on January 19, 1920, Norfolk's streets were flooded with anti-alcohol revelers celebrating their victory. Almost 15,000 jubilant teetotalers joined a parade led by Sunday, who marched next to a 20-foot long black coffin symbolizing the death of demon rum. When the parade ended at a Methodist church, Sunday jumped on top of the coffin, singing hymns and delivering a fire-and-brimstone sermon that rocked the rafters. The next day, Norfolk's 115 bars closed until Prohibition was lifted in 1933.

Virginia Beach & Norfolk

Bad Habits Wing & Oyster Bar

1464 Mount Pleasant Road
Chesapeake, VA 23322
(757) 842-6565

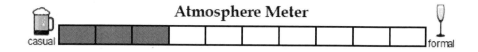

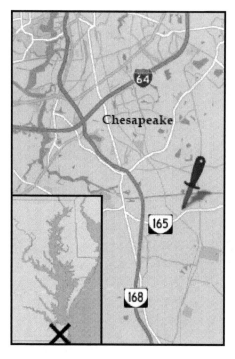

Going to the mall (especially with teenagers) can be a harrowing experience. For some of us, even a quick jaunt to run errands leaves us tense, exhausted and desperate for a rejuvenating beverage.

That's why every shopping center should harbor a place like Bad Habits Wing & Oyster Bar, where the weary and frazzled can find relief. It's the kind of place that transports you from retail agony to beachy peace.

Located between a UPS Store and an urgent care clinic, the front door opens to reveal interior décor that belongs on the waterfront. Wooden tables are shaped like surfboards. Sharks, marlins and trophy fish (caught by a local patron) are mounted on white walls along with framed pictures of crashing waves and colorful beer posters. The atmosphere is upbeat casual, and the bartender extends a warm welcome to newcomers and regulars alike.

Rolls of paper towels on each table offer proof that seafood and Buffalo wings easily coexist, and half the fun of eating them is getting a little messy. Bad Habits doesn't offer an extensive list of oysters, but several local bivalves are served year-round, even in the dog days of summer. James River and Lynnhaven oysters are among the fresh favorites.

The "Sandbar" raw bar steamers present icy platters of specialty oysters, clams, shrimp, and crab legs. Oysters Rockefeller and a jalapeño oyster bake lead the appetizers, along with blackened slices of ahi tuna and creamy crab dip. "Beachbum" po' boys fry to perfection seafood such as oysters, flounder, shrimp and scallops. The famous chicken wings range in heat from Wimpy and Old Bay to more dangerous levels such as Killer, Atomic, and Below Hell. Sandwiches, burgers and salads are also on the menu.

Virginia Beach & Norfolk

McCormick & Schmick's Virginia Beach

211 Market Street
Virginia Beach, VA 23462
(757) 687-8686
www.mccormickandschmicks.com

Atmosphere Meter

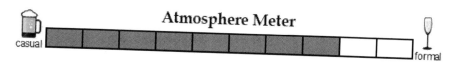

casual — formal

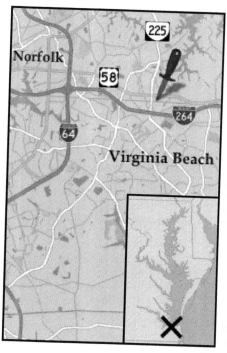

The presence of a McCormick & Schmick's in an up-and-coming area is often an indicator that the local economy is thriving and fine dining has arrived. The M&S in Virginia Beach Town Center is no exception. It's surrounded by quality restaurants, bars, high-end hotels, specialty shops, and chic boutiques.

Plus, it's smack dab in the middle of new entertainment venues. On one side of M&S is the Fountain Plaza, which showcases a gamut of local artists from acoustic guitarists to weekly jazz singers. On the other side is the Sandler Center for Performing Arts. Erected in 2007, this gorgeous cultural facility is home to the symphony and dance groups. The entire area buzzes with excitement about an emerging arts scene just a stone's throw from the beach.

The décor at this M&S location is similar to others in the chain. Waiters in black pants and shirts tend to customers seated in spacious rooms with dark wood walls and art deco chandeliers overhead. A long wooden bar near the entrance entices weary travelers to come inside and quench their thirst. The atmosphere is sedate but inviting.

Tables are laden with seafood from the Chesapeake Bay, Pacific Rim, Atlantic Ocean, and Gulf of Mexico. Connecticut Blue Points appear on the menu, but many oysters are local from the James and Rappahannock rivers and the waters around, Chincoteague Island. When the chef adds heat to the bivalves, the result is a scrumptious platter of buttermilk fried oysters. During a recent happy hour visit, $1 "shrimp and shuck" oysters were served.

Fresh seafood rises to the forefront of the menu, with a wide variety of options such as steamed mussels, blackened snapper, almond-crusted rainbow trout, shrimp stuffed with lump crab meat, and fish and chips. Meat eaters can indulge in steaks, chicken, and burgers.

Bubba's Seafood Restaurant & Crabhouse

3323 Shore Drive
Virginia Beach, VA 23451
(757) 481-3513
www.bubbasseafoodrestaurant.com

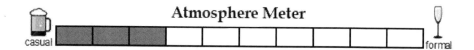

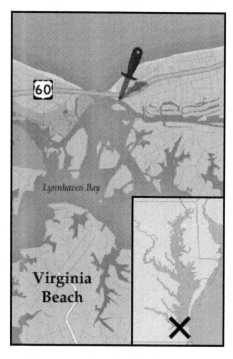

For about 60 years, Bubba's has dished out fresh seafood and offered fantastic views of Lynnhaven River from its two-tiered deck. They usually serve James and Rappahannock River oysters, but Lynnhavens, Chincoteagues and Eastern Shore mollusks, as well as steamed shrimp and clams, also appear at the raw bar. Oysters Rockefeller and Caesar salad with fried oysters are irresistible.

Seafood standouts include Bubba's baked scallops and soft-shell crab dinner. The daily catch — blackened or stuffed — features a lengthy list of local fish such as yellowfin tuna, mahi mahi, flounder, red snapper, trout and rockfish. Bubba burgers, with cheese, bacon, and crab, marry the land and sea inside a bun. The atmosphere is casual and lively, especially on weekends. Boaters take note: A marina and fishing supply store are next door.

The river creates a scenic backdrop, but these waters have undergone turbulent times. Pollution, disease and erosion of tidal wetlands decimated what was among the Chesapeake's biggest and most flavorful oysters.

Good news for oyster lovers: Massive habitat restoration began in earnest about a decade ago, and it's an admirable success story. Spearheaded by Lynnhaven River Now and Chesapeake Bay Foundation, along with residents and watermen, the famous Lynnhaven oyster is making a strong comeback. About 10 years ago, the local oyster population bottomed out to nearly 1% of historic levels. Today it's risen to 10% and still growing, thanks to clean water and land preservation efforts. So, before you dip into a dozen fresh-shucked oysters, give a nod in gratitude to locals who fought hard to save their waterway.

266 Virginia Beach & Norfolk

Dockside Restaurant

3311 Shore Drive
Virginia Beach, VA 23451
(757) 481-4545
www.docksideva.com

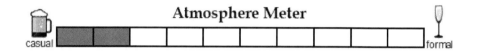

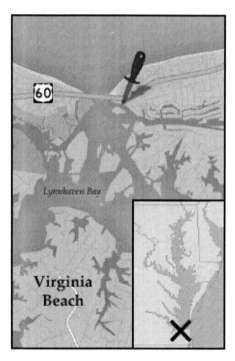

When you're on the prowl for oysters and adventure, head to Dockside Restaurant where eating is only half the fun. From here you can spend the day on a charter boat fishing for flounder, rockfish, bluefish or whatever local delicacy swims your way. If you'd rather watch than catch, you can take a sunset cruise to see dolphins play in their natural habitat. Want the seagull's perspective? Then sign up for a para-sailing trip that gets you airborne above the surf and sand.

This much excitement can rustle up a hearty appetite, so take a seat on the back deck of this charming restaurant where sunsets over the water are spectacular. Its vibe is relaxed, and the interior bamboo and wooden walls are decorated with mounted sports fish and model sailboats. Live music on weekends underscores the easy getaway feeling.

Shuckers pop open Lynnhaven, Seaside, and Sewansecott oysters, but other local bivalves are known to slide onto the raw bar list along with shrimp, clams and crabs. Oysters Rockefeller and clams casino are the main mollusks among the appetizers. Fried oysters, stuffed shrimp and snow crab legs garner high marks from the dinner crowd. Pasta, chicken, steaks, burgers and sandwiches accommodate carnivores, while the kids' menu takes care of your little guppy's whims. Budget-conscious diners who arrive before 5:30 can save some cash with a discounted Sunset Special.

If all this isn't enough to quench your thirst for Lynnhaven's finest, step into Dockside's award-winning seafood market. It's stocked with more than 1,000 different bottles of wine, snacks, seasonings and a wide variety of just-caught fish unloaded daily by local watermen.

Virginia Beach & Norfolk

Chick's Oyster Bar

2143 Vista Circle
Virginia Beach, VA 23451
(757) 481-5757
www.chicksoysterbar.com

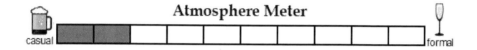

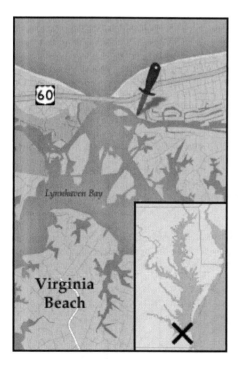

Where does eating oysters feel like an endless beach party? At Chick's Oyster Bar on the Lynnhaven River. The house features two oysters — James River and Seaside Salty — and the kitchen turns that seafood duo into a bivalve lover's bonanza.

For starters, you can get 59 cent oysters at Happy Hour, along with bargain rate clams, wings, beer, and orange or margarita crushes. The potent oyster shooters are a timeless tradition.

The menu's showstopper is Oysters Redneck Way, a baked delight with seasoned collard greens, pimento cheese, crispy bacon and jalapeño peppers. Fried oysters come on a platter or in a sandwich. Other dishes pulled from the sea include crab cakes, fried shrimp, crunchy calamari and seared tuna bites. The brunch menu's Lynnhaven Seafood Omelet with shrimp, crab, cheese and peppers cries out for a good-morning Bloody Mary. Chick's Oyster Roast & Pig Pickin' is a must-attend autumn event.

Chick's is a sprawling place, boisterous and fun, with one room flowing into the next. A menagerie of colorful nautical items, trophy fish, surfboards and crabs are tacked on the walls above cherry-red leather booths. Wooden decks facing the water set the stage for unbridled merriment.

It's fitting that a black-and-white skull and crossbones flag hangs from the rafters in the bar. Lynnhaven's hidden inlets were ideal hiding spots for 18th century pirates, and the close proximity to the Atlantic gave buccaneers an easy escape from authorities. Blackbeard was infamous for looting ships and plundering towns along these shores. Also nearby, the nefarious French pirate Louis Guittar was captured after a fierce maritime battle with Virginia's Governor Nicholson.

Virginia Beach & Norfolk

Lynnhaven Fish House Restaurant

2350 Starfish Road
Virginia Beach, VA 23451
(757) 481-0003
www.lynnhavenfishhouse.net

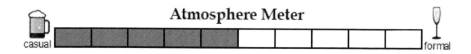

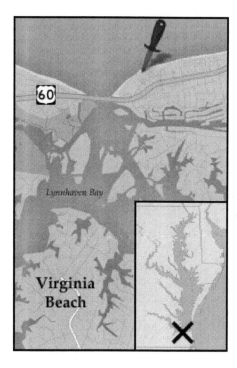

The best time to visit Lynnhaven Fish House Restaurant is during the high oyster season in autumn and winter. That's when its chef scours the James River and the Maryland and Virginia Eastern Shore for bivalves from the Chesapeake's inlets, tributary rivers and Atlantic waters. His goal is to create a perfect balance between the buttery and briny taste experience. In the heat of summer, when wild local oysters focus on reproducing and their size diminishes, the restaurant only carries a few.

Year-round the menu offers lightly battered and fried oysters and a classic Rockefeller, along with half-shell or steamed clams from the Eastern Shore. Baked Scallops

Lynnhaven is topped with lump crab meat and Gouda cheese. When local watermen bring in the fresh catch of the day, you can ask the kitchen to top the dish with a long laundry list of sauces including mango salsa, sesame-soy, wasabi, champagne-lobster cream, mushroom-wine, Cajun and Mediterranean. Twin lobster tails, Alaskan king crabs and stuffed shrimp imperial are simply scrumptious. The Butcher's Block with steaks, pork chops and chicken round out dining options for carnivores.

Since 1978, the Kyrus family has owned this seaside spot and created a welcoming environment for guests. Window seats offer a picturesque view of hopeful fishermen dropping their lines from the pier next door. Above the bar area is a huge stained-glass compass that sends a bold splash of color across the ceiling. Hand-painted murals throughout the restaurant depict scenes of daily life in this charming waterfront community. Red cushioned chairs with matching red cloth napkins set the tone for casual elegance in the spacious dining room.

Lucky Oyster Seafood Grill

2165 General Booth Boulevard
Virginia Beach, VA 23454
(757) 430-9600
www.luckyoystervb.com

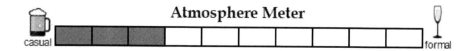

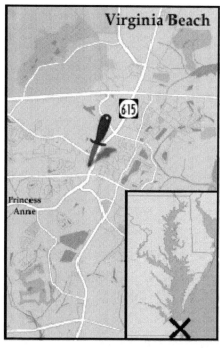

Any restaurant with oysters of the week and beers of the month sounds like a lucky place to be. That's what's in store for you at Lucky Oyster Seafood Grill.

During a recent visit in August, the bartender presented a sheet of paper touting three fresh oysters — Misty Points, Watch House Points and Duxburys — and promised more would be on her list in the fall.

Washing down a dozen on the half shell with monthly special beers such as Blue Moon White IPA makes customers feel pretty lucky. The raw bar looks like Bay seafood nirvana. Every day the icy display is packed with Chesapeake oysters, Eastern Shore clams, steamed shrimp and crab legs. No wonder it's won Best of the Beach Raw Bar six times since opening in 2007.

Cooked oysters run the gamut from oyster stew with applewood bacon, onions and celery to fried oyster platters and Cajun fried oyster burgers with asiago cheese on top. Fresh catch dishes take advantage of plentiful local seafood including sesame-seared wasabi tuna, blackened mahi mahi, fried scallops, crab-stuffed flounder and pecan-crusted tilapia. Burgers, steaks and chicken are on hand for meat eaters.

In addition to good hearty food, the place has an energetic atmosphere that celebrates the traditions of Chesapeake watermen. Brick walls are decorated with fishing nets, lures, buoys and poles along with vintage signs for famous Bay ports such as Oxford, Annapolis, and Norfolk. Simple wooden tables fill the spacious rooms, and two tables rest inside the stern of a former boat called the *Canyon Express*. It's the kind of busy place where you'd feel comfortable bringing your children for dinner or just hanging out at the bar listening to regulars share local lore. The outdoor patio is the sweet spot for breezy summer days.

Virginia Beach & Norfolk

Metropolitan Oyster Exchange

972 Laskin Road
Virginia Beach, VA 23451
(757) 222-2202
www.metropolitanoysterexchange.com

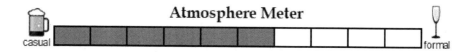

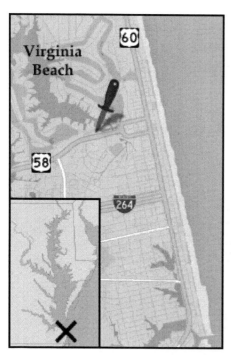

Some might disagree, but the premium seats at Metropolitan Oyster Exchange are at the shucking station. Sure, you can nestle into a cushy booth and enjoy the pastel gray walls, dim lights and contemporary décor. And the patio out front is pleasant on a warm spring evening. But die-hard oyster crusaders want to be where the action is — and that's with the shucker.

Once you get settled on a stool, the shucker suggests a specialty cocktail. In his repertoire are libations ranging from the classic Sidecar to modern drinks such as I Reckon (Rittenhouse rye, apple brandy, honey and prosecco). Behind the shucker hangs a chalkboard heralding the oysters du jour. During our visit, Hungars Creeks, Sewansecotts and Bogues Bays complimented the house standards from the bayside of the

Eastern Shore and Atlantics from Magothy Bay. While splitting open your bivalves, the shucker explains where they're grown and how they taste on a scale of buttery to briny. By the time the half shells are laid out on a silver tray of ice, you feel like a master ready to receive your bounty.

Chilled middleneck clams, shrimp and lobster complete the raw bar options. Appetizer highlights include oysters Rockefeller, steamed mussels, smoked whitefish spread and fried calamari. The roasted beet salad with fried goat cheese and arugula is crisp and savory. Entrees include a litany of favorites including seafood tacos, fried oysters, blackened catfish and shrimp with grits. Sandwiches and po' boys provide casual fare, while steaks, chicken breasts, grilled cheese with pork belly and burgers cater to carnivores.

In truth, no matter where you sit, you're destined for an exquisitely prepared meal and a memorable dining experience peppered with outstanding service and a welcoming vibe.

Virginia Beach & Norfolk

Catch 31 Fish House & Bar

3001 Atlantic Avenue
Virginia Beach, VA 23451
(757) 213-3474
www.catch31.com

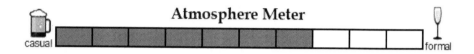

With the mighty Neptune statue standing guard next door, music wafting from the pavilion, and the sound of waves tumbling over the sand, it's easy to fall in love with Catch 31. During the day you can amble through lush tropical plants, settle into a white beach chair and soak up the sun. In the evening, it's a cozy spot to sip a nightcap by crackling firepits and admire the sparkling lights wrapped around palm tree trunks. The restaurant interior is lovely as well, with a large ship-shaped bar, a long open kitchen and spacious sophisticated dining rooms accented with cobalt blue glassware resting on top of smooth wooden tables.

But if you're on a quest for oysters, your heart starts thumping the moment you lay eyes on the daily specials board. Under the heading "Today's Daily Oyster Harvest" are 21 different brands of bivalves from across North America. Representatives from the Chesapeake region include James River, Rappahannock, Sewansecott, Lynnhaven and Shooting Point oysters. Counterparts from northern waters include Wellfleets, Blue Points and Malpeques.

This bivalve bonanza belongs to Hilton, but it doesn't feel like a hotel restaurant and the food doesn't taste like it's from an industrial kitchen. Quite the contrary. Dishes are fresh, local and prepared flawlessly. Steamed and sautéed seafood standouts include Prince Edward Island mussels, coastal middleneck clams and peel-and-eat shrimp. With a pledge to go from dock to table, the daily catch is delivered whole by watermen around the Tidewater region and filleted in-house by Catch 31 cooks. Atlantic Coast tuna, snapper, swordfish and mahi mahi are among the favorites. Wood-grilled steaks are available for meat eaters, and craft beers are chosen from Virginia Beach, Hampton and Norfolk breweries.

Rudee's Restaurant & Cabana Bar

227 Mediterranean Avenue
Virginia Beach, VA 23451
(757) 425-1777
www.rudees.com

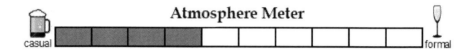

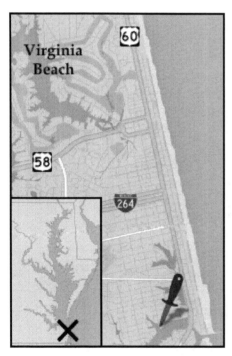

Imagine sitting in a covered wooden glider seat at a scenic marina watching a ruby red sunset over the water. Laughter fills the air, and a waiter gently places a cold beverage in your hand to toast the day's end. That's what life is like at Rudee's.

The Cabana Bar is an idyllic place to escape the daily grind and the perfect vantage point for watching fishermen unload their catch. The main building, which started as the marina's bait and tackle shop, was renovated in the style of an old Coast Guard station. Floor-to-ceiling windows guarantee a gorgeous view. The atmosphere is laid back, and merriment is contagious.

Across from the bar stands the shucking station, which is sure to catch every oyster lover's attention. Watermen from the Chesapeake Bay and Atlantic Coast pack the raw bar with a cornucopia of local seafood. Shooting Point Oysters from Virginia's Eastern Shore line up with littleneck clams, Carolina shrimp and Alaskan snow crab legs.

Since 1983, Rudee's has been an epicenter for food and fun at the beach, and the menu reflects its dedication to Poseidon's treasures. Oysters Rockefeller, Cajun sea scallops and Hatteras clam chowder rank among the appetizer favorites. Irresistible entrees include seafood alfredo laced with shrimp and scallops and fresh fish Chesapeake style topped with jumbo lump crab meat, Smithfield ham and béarnaise sauce. If your group is divided between dishes from the land or sea, Rudee's can accommodate every whim. Some can pick fried oysters, blackened tuna sandwiches or Maine lobster rolls. Others can dig into pork BBQ on a bun, juicy burgers or Buffalo chicken sandwiches. It's all about easy living and good times along this charming seaside inlet.

Chesapeake Aquafarms & Oyster Brands

Chesapeake Oyster Lovers Handbook

282 Oyster Aquafarms & Brands

The 13 Oyster Growing Zones of the Chesapeake Bay

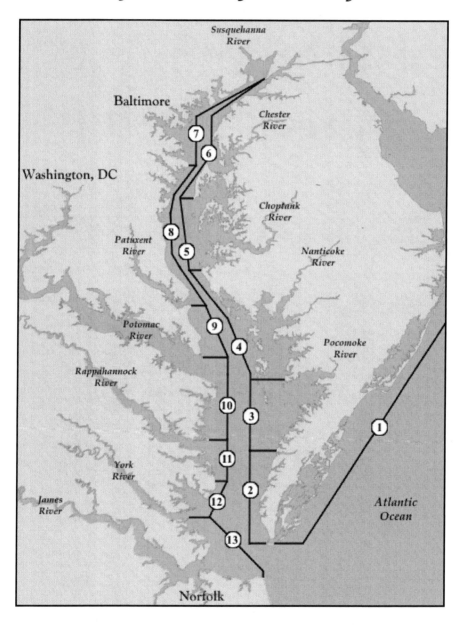

The 13 Oyster Growing Zones of the Chesapeake Bay

Oyster Growing Zone	Salinity Range	Zone Description
1-Seaside Zone	28-32 ppt	East from Cape Charles, north along the Eastern Shore's Atlantic coast
2-Cape Charles Zone	18-22 ppt	West from Occohannock Creek, south along the Eastern Shore's Chesapeake Bay to Cape Charles
3-Pocomoke River Zone	16-18 ppt	West from Tangier Island, south along the Eastern Shore's Chesapeake Bay to Occohannock Creek
4-Nanticoke River Zone	15-18 ppt	West from Taylors Island, south along the Eastern Shore's Chesapeake Bay to Tangier Island
5-Choptank River Zone	12-15 ppt	West from southernmost point of Kent Island, south along the Eastern Shore's Chesapeake Bay to Taylors Island
6-Chester River Zone	1-13 ppt	Southwest from Turkey Point on Elk Neck, south along the Eastern Shore's Chesapeake Bay to southernmost point of Kent Island
7-Susquehanna River Zone	1-10 ppt	Southwest from Turkey Point on Elk Neck, south along the Western Shore to Sandy Point
8-Patuxent River Zone	10-17 ppt	East from Sandy Point, south along the Western Shore to Cedar Point
9-Southern Maryland Zone	15-18 ppt	East from Cedar Point, south along the Western Shore to Point Lookout
10-Potomac River Zone	10-17 ppt	East from Point Lookout, south along the Western Shore to Windmill Point
11-Rappahannock River Zone	16-18 ppt	East from Windmill Point, south along the Western Shore to the midpoint of the Middle Peninsula
12-York River Zone	16-18 ppt	East from midpoint of the Middle Peninsula, south along the Western Shore to Goodwin Island
13-James River Zone	16-30 ppt	Southeast from Goodwin Island, west along the Tidewater to Cape Henry

American Shellfish Company

P.O. Box 138, Cheriton, VA 23316
(757) 678-3301
www.americanshellfish.com

Brands: Cape Charles Carpe Diem Premium Oysters, Chincoteague Atlantics Choice Oysters
Growing Regions: 1-Seaside Zone, 2-Cape Charles Zone

Anderson's Neck Oyster Company

1696 Cherry Row Lane, Shacklefords, VA 23156
(804) 396-6680
www.andersonsneck.com

Brand: Eagle Flats
Growing Region: 12-York River Zone

Ballard Fish & Oyster Company

1588 Townfield Drive, Cheriton, VA 23316
(757) 331-1208
www.ballardfish.com

Brands: Chincoteague Cultured Salt Oysters, Chunu Cultured Oysters, Misty Point Oysters, Watch House Point Oysters

Growing Regions: 1-Seaside Zone, 2-Cape Charles Zone

Barren Island Oyster Company

Hoopers Island, MD 21634
(917) 584-8029
www.barrenislandoysters.com

Brands: Barren Island Oysters, Fat Beech Oysters, Ugly Oysters

Growing Region: 4-Nanticoke River Zone

Bay Landing Shellfish Company

P.O. Box 1475, Berlin, MD 21811
(443) 614-3164
www.baylandingshellfish.com

Brand: Mojo Oysters
Growing Region: 1-Seaside Zone

Bevans Oyster Company

1090 Skipjack Road, Kinsale, VA 22488
(804) 472-2331
www.bevansoyster.com

Brand: Bevans Oysters
Growing Region: 10-Potomac River Zone

Big Island Aquaculture

2149 Big Island View Road, Gloucester, VA 23072
(757) 759-7661
www.bigislandaquaculture.com

Brand: Big Island Oysters
Growing Region: 12-York River Zone

Broadwater Oyster Company

Broadwater Circle, Oyster, VA 23419
(302) 542-4465
www.broadwateroysters.com

Brands: Broadwater Oysters, Little Bitches, Saxis Island Bullets
Growing Region: 1-Seaside Zone, 2-Cape Charles Zone, 3-Pocomoke River Zone

Chapel Creek Oyster Company

311 Hallieford Road, Cobbs Creek, VA 23035
(804) 815-6132
www.shuckum.com

Brand: Chapel Creek Oysters
Growing Region: 11-Rappahannock River Zone

Cherrystone Aqua-Farms

1588 Townfield Drive, Cheriton, VA 23316
(757) 331-1208
www.cherrystoneaqua-farms.com

Brand: Watch House Point Oysters
Growing Region: 2-Cape Charles Zone

Chesapeake Bay Oyster Company

P.O. Box 96, Wake, VA 23176
(804) 776-0220
www.bayoyster.com

Brand: Parrot Island Oysters
Growing Region: 11-Rappahannock River Zone

Chessie Seafood & Aquafarms

P.O. Box 412, Wicomico, VA 23184
(804) 815-7982
www.yorkriveroysters.com

Brand: York River Oysters
Growing Region: 12-York River Zone

Chincoteague Shellfish Farms

7564 Eastside Road, Chincoteague, VA 23336
(757) 336-1985
www.clamandoyster.com
Brands: Chincoteague Cultured Salt Oysters, Chunu Cultured Oysters, Misty Point Oysters
Growing Region: 1-Seaside Zone

Premium Farm Raised Oysters
from The Chesapeake Bay

The Choptank Oyster Company

6035 Castle Haven Road, Cambridge, MD 21613
(410) 221-7900
www.marineticsinc.com
Brand: Choptank Sweets
Growing Region: 5-Choptank River Zone

Oyster Aquafarms & Brands **291**

Circle C Oyster Ranch

49676 Freeman's Road, Dameron, MD 20628
(301) 872-4177
www.oysterranching.com

Brand: Lineback Oysters
Growing Region: 9-Southern Maryland Zone

Daily Oyster Company

Seaford, VA 23696
(757) 759-4058
www.dailyoystercompany.com

Brand: Bay Breeze Oysters
Growing Region: 12-York River Zone

Deltaville Oyster Company

210 Circle Drive, Deltaville, VA 23043
(804) 357-1931
www.deltavilleoystercompany.com

Brand: NautiGirl Oysters
Growing Region: 11-Rappahannock River Zone

Double T Oyster Ranch

18521 Herring Creek Road, Tall Timbers, MD 20690
(301) 994-1508
www.ttoyster.com

Brand: Double T Oysters
Growing Region: 10-Potomac River Zone

DRAGON CREEK S&P, LLC

Dragon Creek Seafood & Oyster Company

Montross, VA 22520
(703) 625-0599

Brand: Hayden's Reef Oysters
Growing Region: 10-Potomac River Zone

Fat 'N Happy Oyster Company

51 Railway Drive, Heathsville, VA 22473
(804) 761-0908

Brand: Fat 'N Happy Oysters
Growing Region: 10-Potomac River Zone

Oyster Aquafarms & Brands

Goodwin Island Oyster Company

209 Belvin Lane, Yorktown, VA 23692
(757) 725-5538
www.goodwinislandoystercompany.com

Brands: Dandylicious Oysters, Sea-Licious Oysters, Yorkster Oysters

Growing Region: 12-York River Zone

The Great Wicomico Oyster Company

191 Bow Wood Drive, Heathsville, VA 22473
(443) 261-4963
www.greatwicomicooyster.com

Brands: Double Dee Oysters, Skipjack Oysters, Sweet Petites

Growing Region: 10-Potomac River Zone

Hayes Oyster Company

4564 Beacon Hill Drive, Williamsburg, VA 23188
(757) 707-0799
www.hayesoystercompany.com

Brand: Gloucester Point Oysters
Growing Region: 12-York River Zone

H.M. Terry Company

5039 Willis Wharf Road, Willis Wharf, VA 23486
(757) 442-7006
www.hmterry.com

Brand: Sewansecott Oysters
Growing Region: 1-Seaside Zone

Hollywood Oyster Company

P.O. Box 575, Hollywood, MD 20636
(301) 710-6396
www.hollywoodoyster.com
Brands: Hollywood Oysters, Sweet Jesus Oysters
Growing Region: 8-Patuxent River Zone

Honga Oyster Company

2012 Wingate Bishops Head Road, Toddville, MD 21672
(240) 447-4500
www.hongaoyster.com
Brand: HongaTonk Oysters
Growing Region: 4-Nanticoke River Zone

Oyster Aquafarms & Brands

Hoopers Island Oyster Aquaculture Company

2500 Old House Point Road, Fishing Creek, MD 21634
(410) 397-3664
www.cgoysters.com

Brands: Chesapeake Gold Oysters, Holy Grail Oysters, Whitewood Cove Oysters
Growing Region: 4-Nanticoke River Zone

J.C. Walker Brothers

12459 Ballard Drive, Willis Wharf, VA 23486
(757) 442-6000
www.jcwalkerbrosclams.com

Brand: Revel's Island Bay Oysters
Growing Region: 1-Seaside Zone

Oyster Aquafarms & Brands

Johnny Oyster Seed Company

5223 Williams Wharf Road, St. Leonard, MD 20685
(410) 610-1508
www.johnnyoysterseed.com

Brand: Calvert Crest Oysters
Growing Region: 8-Patuxent River Zone

Joyner Brothers Oysters

771 Poquoson Avenue, Poquoson, VA 223662
(757) 592-3728

Brand: Poquoson Oysters
Growing Region: 12-York River Zone

Oyster Aquafarms & Brands **299**

Little Wicomico Oyster Company

4990 Hacks Neck Road, Heathsville, VA 22473
(804) 436-5962

Brand: Little Wicomico Oysters
Growing Region: 10-Potomac River Zone

Ludford Brothers Oyster Company

4425 Delmar Drive, Virginia Beach, VA 23455
(757) 663-6970
www.pleasurehouseoysters.com

Brand: Pleasure House Oysters
Growing Region: 13-James River Zone

Oyster Aquafarms & Brands

Lynnhaven Bay Aquaculture Oysters

P.O. Box 937, Cheriton, VA 23316
(757) 263-7599

Brand: Church Point Oysters
Growing Region: 13-James River Zone

Lynnhaven Oyster Company

2605 Moss Road, Virginia Beach, VA 23451
(757) 228-1522
www.lynnhavenoystercompany.com

Brand: Lynnhaven Oysters
Growing Region: 13-James River Zone

Lynnhaven River Oyster Company

3706 Surry Road, Virginia Beach, VA 23455
(757) 406-0606

Brand: Lynnhaven River Oysters
Growing Region: 13-James River Zone

Madhouse Oysters

2405 Hoopers Island Road, Fishing Creek, MD 21634
(410) 310-4132
www.madhouseoysters.com

Brands: Black Horse Oysters, Madhouse Oysters
Growing Region: 4-Nanticoke River Zone

Main Stream Oysters

3166 Main Street, Chincoteague, VA 23336
(757) 336-3522

Brand: Main Stream Oysters
Growing Region: 1-Seaside Zone

Premium Farm Raised Oysters
from The Chesapeake Bay

Marinetics, Inc.

6035 Castle Haven Road, Cambridge, MD 21613
(410) 221-7900
www.marineticsinc.com

Brand: Choptank Sweets
Growing Region: 5-Choptank River Zone

MiFarm Oysters

234 Mifarm Road, White Stone, VA 22578
(804) 435-3077
www.mifarmoysters.com

Brand: Fleet's Bay Oysters
Growing Region: 11-Rappahannock River Zone

Nandua Oyster Company

13348 Full Measure Lane, Pungoteague, VA 23422
(757) 442-7742

Brand: Nandua Oysters
Growing Region: 3-Pocomoke River Zone

New Point Oyster Company

P.O. Box 35, New Point, VA 23125
(703) 408-2035

Brand: New Point Oysters
Growing Region: 12-York River Zone

Ocean Cove Seafood

P.O. Box 197, Capeville, VA 23313
(757) 331-1750
www.oceancoveclams.com

Brand: Indian Rock Oysters
Growing Region: 1-Seaside Zone

Orchard Point Oyster Company

24179 Walnut Point Road, Chestertown, MD 21620
(443) 480-0302
www.orchardpointoysters.com

Brand: Orchard Point Oysters
Growing Region: 6-Chester River Zone

Patuxent Seafood Company

4149 School Road, Broomes Island, MD 20615
(410) 610-5395
www.patuxentseafood.com

Brand: Island Girl Oysters
Growing Region: 8-Patuxent River Zone

Pepper Creek Shellfish Farm

4956 New Point Comfort Highway, Port Haywood, VA 23138
(800) 721-8432
www.peppercreekshellfishfarm.com
Brand: Pepper Creek Oysters
Growing Region: 12-York River Zone

Point Lookout Oyster Company

50525 Scotland Beach Road, Scotland, MD 20687
www.pointlookoutoystercompany.com
Brand: Point Lookout Oysters
Growing Region: 9-Southern Maryland Zone

Rappahannock Oyster Company

784 Locklies Creek Road, Topping, VA 23169
(804) 204-1709
www.rroysters.com

Brands: Barcat Oysters, Old Black Salts, Olde Salts, Rappahannock River Oysters, Snow Hill Oysters, Stingray Oysters, Witch Duck Oysters

Growing Regions: 1-Seaside Zone, 11-Rappahannock River Zone, 12-York River Zone, 13-James River Zone

Ruby Salts Oyster Company

2132 Cherrystone Road, Cape Charles, VA 23310
(757) 331-1495
www.rubysalts.com

Brand: Ruby Salts Oysters
Growing Region: 2-Cape Charles Zone

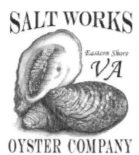

Salt Works Oyster Company

7264 Otter Road, Franktown, VA 23354
(757) 442-4455

Brand: Salt Works Oysters
Growing Region: 2-Cape Charles Zone

Sandy Point Shellfish

P.O. Box 1262, Eastville, VA 23347
(757) 678-6146

Brand: Sandy Point Oysters
Growing Region: 2-Cape Charles Zone

Sapidus Farms

1345 Bogey Neck Road, Heathsville, VA 22473
(443) 864-3600
www.sapidusfarms.com

Brand: Happy Oysters
Growing Region: 10-Potomac River Zone

Seaford Oyster Company

P.O. Box 602, Seaford, VA 23696
(757) 268-2719
www.seafordoyster.com

Brand: Seaford Oysters
Growing Region: 12-York River Zone

Ship Point Oyster Company

512 Wildey Road, Seaford, VA 23696
(757) 848-3557

Brand: Ship Point Oysters
Growing Region: 12-York River Zone

Shooting Point Oyster Company

5456 Bayford Road, Franktown, VA 23354
(757) 693-1303
www.shootingpointoysters.com

Brands: Avery's Pearls, Nassawadox Salts, Shooting Point Salts
Growing Regions: 1-Seaside Zone, 2-Cape Charles Zone

Oyster Aquafarms & Brands 311

Shore Seafood

19424 Saxis Road, VA 23427
(757) 824-5517
www.shoreseafoodinc.com

Brand: Grand Pearl Oysters
Growing Region: 3-Pocomoke River Zone

Shore Thing Shellfish

P.O. Box 74, Tall Timbers, MD 20690
(240) 538-1336
www.shorethingshellfish.com

Brand: Shore Thing Oysters
Growing Region: 10-Potomac River Zone

Shores & Ruark Seafood Company

453 Johnsons Drive, Urbanna, VA 23175
(804) 758-5640
www.shoresandruark.com

Brands: Choice of Chesapeake Bay Oysters, Urbanna Creek Oysters
Growing Region: 11-Rappahannock River Zone

Stump Cove Oyster Company

5559 Morris Neck Road, Cambridge, MD 21613
(443) 324-0354
stumpcove.weebly.com

Brand: Stump Cove Oysters
Growing Region: 5-Choptank River Zone

Tangier Sound Oyster Company

6198 Bob Horsey Road, Marion Station, MD 21838
(410) 623-3816
Brand: Uncle Ernie's Oysters
Growing Region: 4-Nanticoke River Zone

Tarkill Aquaculture Ventures

14008 Tarkill Road, Onancock, VA 23417
(757) 894-2009
www.tarkillaquacultureventures.com
Brands: McKinney's Island Oysters,
Ropewalk Liberty Oysters
Growing Region: 3-Pocomoke River Zone

38° North Oysters

P.O. Box 2, Scotland, MD 20687
(301) 872-5051
www.38northoysters.com

Brand: 38° North Oysters
Growing Region: 9-Southern Maryland Zone

Tilghman Island Oyster Farm

Tilghman, MD 21671
(410) 302-9861
www.tilghmanislandoysterfarm.com

Brand: Black Walnut Point Oysters
Growing Region: 5-Choptank River Zone

Oyster Aquafarms & Brands **315**

Toby Island Bay Oyster Farm

5398 Main Street, Chincoteague, VA 23336
(202) 258-9700
www.tobyislandbayoysters.com
Brands: Black Pearl Oysters, Toby Island Oysters
Growing Region: 1-Seaside Zone

Tom's Cove Aquafarms

P.O. Box 355, Chincoteague, VA 23336
(757) 336-1945
www.tomscove.net
Brand: Tom's Cove Oysters
Growing Region: 1-Seaside Zone

True Chesapeake Oyster Company

49944 Airedele Road, Ridge, MD 20680
(301) 363-4880
www.trueoyster.com

Brands: Huckleberry Oysters, M&S Charmer Oysters, Skinny Dipper Oysters
Growing Region: 9-Southern Maryland Zone

War Shore Oyster Company

8229 Boone Boulevard, Vienna, VA 22182
(443) 842-1977
www.warshore.com

Brands: Battle Creek Oysters, Cannon Cove Oysters, War Shore Oysters
Growing Regions: 1-Seaside Zone, 3-Pocomoke River Zone, 12-York River Zone

Ward Oyster Company

6578 Jarvis Road, Gloucester, VA 23061
(804) 693-0044
www.wardoyster.com

Brand: Lone Point Oysters, Mobjack Bay Oysters
Growing Region: 12-York River Zone

W.E. Kellum Seafood

P.O. Box 249, Weems, VA 22576
(804) 438-5476
www.kellumseafood.com

Brand: Kellum Oysters
Growing Region: 11-Rappahannock River Zone

White Stone Oyster Company

202 Route 661, White Stone, VA 22578
(804) 729-5745
www.whitestoneoysters.com

Brand: White Stone Oysters
Growing Region: 11-Rappahannock River Zone

Wild Country Seafood

124 Bay Shore Avenue, Annapolis, MD 21403
(410) 267-6711
www.wildcountryseafood.com

Brand: Patty's Fatty's
Growing Region: 8-Patuxent River Zone

Oyster Aquafarms & Brands **319**

Windmill Point Oyster Company

261 Osprey Lane, White Stone, VA 22578
(804) 577-3179
www.windmilloysters.com

Brand: Windmill Point Oysters
Growing Region: 11-Rappahannock River Zone

Windmill Point Seafood Company

4353 Windmill Point Road, White Stone, VA 22578
(804) 480-9773
www.windmillpointseafood.com

Brand: Fleets Island Oysters
Growing Region: 11-Rappahannock River Zone

Winter Harbor Oysters

Winter Harbor Oysters
6045 Shady Oak Court, Mechanicsville, VA 23111
(804) 212-5169
www.winterharboroysters.com

Brand: Winter Harbor Oysters
Growing Region: 12-York River Zone

Index

A

AJ's on the Creek 142
All Set Restaurant & Bar 110
American Shellfish
    Company 284
Anderson's Neck Oyster
    Company 284
Apropoe's 36
Avery's Pearls 310, 331
A.W. Shucks Raw Bar &
    Grill 256
Awful Arthur's Seafood
    Company 126

B

Bad Habits Wing & Oyster
    Bar 260
Ballard Fish & Oyster
    Company 285
Barcat Oysters 307, 331
Barren Island Oyster
    Company 285
Barren Island Oysters 285, 331
Battle Creek Oysters 316, 331
Bay Breeze Oysters 291, 331
Bay Landing Shellfish
    Company 286
Berret's Seafood Restaurant &
    Taphouse Grill 248
Bevans Oyster Company 286
Bevans Oysters 286, 331
Big Easy Oyster Bar 258
Big Island Aquaculture 287
Big Island Oysters 287, 331

Black Horse Oysters 301, 331
Black Pearl Oysters 315, 331
Black Walnut Point
    Oysters 314, 331
Black's Bar & Kitchen 104
BlackSalt Fish Market &
    Restaurant 150
Blackwall Hitch Alexandria 230
Blackwall Hitch Annapolis 90
Blue Point Provision
    Company 136
BoatHouse Canton 50
Boatyard Bar & Grill 94
Brasserie Brightwell 128
Brew River Restaurant 138
BRINE 208
Broadwater Oyster
    Company 287
Broadwater Oysters 287, 331
Bubba's Seafood Restaurant &
    Crabhouse 264

C

Calvert Crest Oysters 298, 331
Cannon Cove Oysters 316, 332
Cape Charles Carpe Diem
    Premium Oysters 284, 332
Carpe Diem Oysters 284, 332
Carrol's Creek Waterfront
    Restaurant 92
Catch 15 Restaurant & Oyster
    Bar 180
Catch 31 Fish House & Bar 276
Catonsville Gourmet Market &
    Fine Foods 62

Index

Chapel Creek Oyster
  Company 288
Chapel Creek Oysters 288, 332
Cherrystone Aqua-Farms 288
Chesapeake Bay Oyster
  Company 289
Chesapeake Gold
  Oysters 297, 332
Chessie Seafood &
  Aquafarms 289
Chick's Oyster Bar 268
Chincoteague Atlantics Choice
  Oysters 284, 332
Chincoteague Cultured Salt
  Oysters 285, 290, 332
Chincoteague Shellfish
  Farms 290
Choice of Chesapeake Bay
  Oysters 312, 332
Choptank Oyster Company 290
Choptank Sweets 290, 302, 332
Chunu Cultured
  Oysters 285, 290, 332
Church Point Oysters 300, 332
Circle C Oyster Ranch 291
Clyde's at Mark Center 218
Clyde's of Gallery Place 190
Clyde's of Tysons Corner 204
Clyde's Tower Oaks Lodge 100
Columbia Firehouse Restaurant
  & Barroom 226
Crabtown Raw Bar & Grille 252

D

Daily Oyster Company 291
Dandylicious Oysters 294, 332
Deltaville Oyster Company 292
Denson's Grocery & R&B
  Oyster Bar 238
District Commons 166

Dockside Restaurant 266
Double Dee Oysters 294, 332
Double T Oyster Ranch 292
Double T Oysters 292, 332
Dragon Creek Seafood & Oyster
  Company 293

E

Eagle Flats 284, 333
Eat the Rich 174

F

Faidley Seafood 24
Fat 'N Happy Oyster
  Company 293
Fat 'N Happy Oysters 293, 333
Fat Beech Oysters 285, 333
Fiola Mare 158
Fish Market Restaurant & Raw
  Bar 232
Fleet's Bay Oysters 303, 333
Fleets Island Oysters 319, 333
Food Wine & Co. 108

G

Gloucester Point
  Oysters 295, 333
Goodwin Island Oyster
  Company 294
Grand Pearl Oysters 311, 333
Great Wicomico Oyster
  Company 294
Grille 620 60
Grilled Oyster Company 102
GrillMarX Restaurant & Raw
  Bar 98
Gryphon 168

H

Hank's Oyster Bar Capitol Hill 196
Hank's Oyster Bar Dupont Circle 170
Hank's Oyster Bar Old Town .. 224
Happy Oysters 309, 333
Harpoon Larry's Fish House & Oyster Bar 250
Harris Crab House 124
Hayden's Reef Oysters 293, 333
Hayes Oyster Company 295
Heavy Seas Alehouse 42
H.M. Terry Company 295
Hollywood Oyster Company 296
Hollywood Oysters 296, 333
Holy Grail Oysters 297, 333
Honga Oyster Company 296
HongaTonk Oysters 296, 333
Hoopers Island Oyster Aquaculture Company 297
Huckleberry Oysters 316, 333

I

Indian Rock Oysters 304, 333
Island Girl Oysters 305, 333

J

J. Paul's 154
Jackspot 140
J.C. Walker Brothers 297
Jimmie & Sook's Raw Bar & Grill 132
Joe's Seafood, Prime Steak & Stone Crab 182
John W. Faidley Seafood 24
Johnny Oyster Seed Company 298
Johnny's Half Shell 192
Joyner Brother's Oyster Company 298

K

Kellum Oysters 317, 333
Kellum Seafood 317

L

Lee's Landing Dock Bar 74
Legal Sea Foods Restaurant & Oyster Bar Arlington-Crystal City 220
Legal Sea Foods Restaurant & Oyster Bar McLean 206
Legal Sea Foods Restaurant & Oyster Bar Washington 188
Lineback Oysters 291, 334
Little Bitches 287, 334
Little Wicomico Oyster Company 299
Little Wicomico Oysters ... 299, 334
Local Oyster 22
Lone Point Oysters 317, 334
Lucky Oyster Seafood Grill 272
Ludford Brothers Oyster Company 299
Lynnhaven Bay Aquaculture Oysters 300
Lynnhaven Fish House Restaurant 270
Lynnhaven Oyster Company .. 300
Lynnhaven Oysters 300, 334
Lynnhaven River Oyster Company 301
Lynnhaven River Oysters 301, 334

Lyon Hall 216

M

M&S Charmer Oysters 316, 334
Madhouse Oysters 301, 334
Main Stream Oysters 302, 334
Main Street Oyster House 72
Mama's on the Half Shell 52
Marinetics Inc. 302
McCormick & Schmick's
  Arlington 222
McCormick & Schmick's
  Baltimore Inner Harbor 34
McCormick & Schmick's
  Harborside at National
  Harbor 116
McCormick & Schmick's
  McLean 202
McCormick & Schmick's
  Virginia Beach 262
McCormick & Schmick's
  Washington 176
McGarvey's Saloon & Oyster
  Bar 86
McKinney's Island
  Oysters 313, 334
McLoone's Pier House National
  Harbor 114
Merroir 242
Metropolitan Oyster
  Exchange 274
Michael's Café Raw Bar &
  Grill 70
Middleton Tavern 88
MiFarm Oysters 303
Misty Point Oysters .. 285, 290, 334
Mobjack Bay Oysters 317, 334
Mojo Oysters 286, 334
Mt. Washington Tavern 64
Mussel Bar & Grille
  Arlington 214
Mussel Bar & Grille
  Baltimore 44
Mussel Bar & Grille
  Bethesda 106

N

Nandua Oyster Company 303
Nandua Oysters 303, 334
Nassawadox Salts 310, 334
NautiGirl Oysters 292, 334
New Point Oyster Company ... 304
New Point Oysters 304, 335
Nickel Taphouse 66
Nick's Fish House 56
Nick's Oyster Bar 28

O

O'Brien's Oyster Bar &
  Steakhouse 82
Ocean Cove Seafood 304
Ocean Odyssey Restaurant 134
Oceanaire Seafood Room
  Baltimore 40
Oceanaire Seafood Room
  Washington 186
Old Black Salts 307, 335
Old Ebbitt Grill 184
Olde Salts 307, 335
Orange Anchor 160
Orchard Point Oyster
  Company 305
Orchard Point Oysters 305, 335
Overwood 228
Oyster Farm Seafood Eatery at
  Kings Creek 146

P

Parrot Island Oysters 289, 335
Patty's Fatty's 318, 335
Patuxent Seafood Company 305
Pearl Dive Oyster Palace 172
Pepper Creek Oysters 306, 335
Pepper Creek Shellfish Farm ... 306
Phillips Seafood Baltimore 32
P.J. Clarke's DC 178
Pleasure House Oysters ... 299, 335
Plug Ugly's Publick House 54
Point Lookout Oyster
 Company 306
Point Lookout Oysters 306, 335
Pop's SeaBar 152
Poquoson Oysters 298, 335
Rappahannock Oyster Bar 194
Rappahannock Oyster
 Company 307
Rappahannock River
 Oysters 307, 335
Republic 112
Revel's Island Bay
 Oysters 297, 335
Riptide by the Bay 46
Ropewalk Liberty
 Oysters 313, 335
Ruby Salts Oyster Company ... 307
Ruby Salts Oysters 307, 335
Rudee's Restaurant & Cabana
 Bar 278
Rusty Scupper 30
Ryleigh's Oyster Federal Hill 26
Ryleigh's Oyster Hunt Valley 68
Ryleigh's Oyster Mount
 Vernon 20

S

Salt Works Oyster Company ... 308
Salt Works Oysters 308, 335
Sandy Point Oysters 308, 336
Sandy Point Shellfish 308
Sapidus Farms 309
Saxis Island Bullets 287, 336
Sea Catch Restaurant & Raw
 Bar 156
Sea Pearl Restaurant &
 Lounge 210
Seaford Oyster Company 309
Seaford Oysters 309, 336
Sea-Licious Oysters 294, 336
Senart's Oyster & Chop
 House 198
Sequoia 164
Severn Inn 80
Sewansecott Oysters 295, 336
Ship Point Oyster Company 310
Ship Point Oysters 310, 336
Shooting Point Oyster
 Company 310
Shooting Point Salts 310, 336
Shore Seafood 311
Shore Thing Oysters 311, 336
Shore Thing Shellfish 311
Shores & Ruark Seafood
 Company 312
Skinny Dipper Oysters 316, 336
Skipjack Oysters 294, 336
Snow Hill Oysters 307, 336
Steak & Main 76
Stingray Oysters 307, 336
Stoney's Seafood House
 Clarke's Landing 120
Stump Cove Oyster
 Company 312
Stump Cove Oysters 312, 336
Sweet Jesus Oysters 296, 336
Sweet Petites 294, 336

T

Tangier Sound Oyster Company 313
Tarkill Aquaculture Ventures 313
Terry Company 295
Thames Street Oyster House 48
38° North Oysters 314, 336
Tides Inn 240
Tilghman Island Oyster Farm 314
Toby Island Bay Oyster Farm .. 315
Toby Island Oysters 315, 337
Tom's Cove Aquafarms 315
Tom's Cove Oysters 315, 337
Tony & Joe's Seafood Place 162
Trio Grill 212
True Chesapeake Oyster Company 316

U

Ugly Oysters 285, 337
Uncle Ernie's Oysters 313, 337
Union Street Public House 234
Urbanna Creek Oysters 312, 337

V

Village Restaurant 144

W

Walker Brothers 297
Walrus Oyster & Ale House 118
War Shore Oyster Company ... 316
War Shore Oysters 316, 337
Ward Oyster Company 317
Washington Street Pub & Oyster Bar 130
Watch House Point Oysters 285, 288, 337
W.E. Kellum Seafood 317
White Stone Oyster Company 318
White Stone Oysters 318, 337
Whitewood Cove Oysters 297, 337
Wild Country Seafood 318
Windmill Point Oyster Company 319
Windmill Point Oysters 319, 337
Windmill Point Seafood Company 319
Winter Harbor Oysters 320, 337
Wit & Wisdom 38
Witch Duck Oysters 307, 337
Woodberry Kitchen 18

Y

Yellowtail at the Market House 84
York River Oyster Company ... 244
York River Oysters 289, 337
Yorkster Oysters 294, 337
Yorktown Pub 246

Chesapeake Oyster Taste Chart

Chesapeake Oyster Lovers Handbook

The 13 Oyster Growing Zones of the Chesapeake Bay

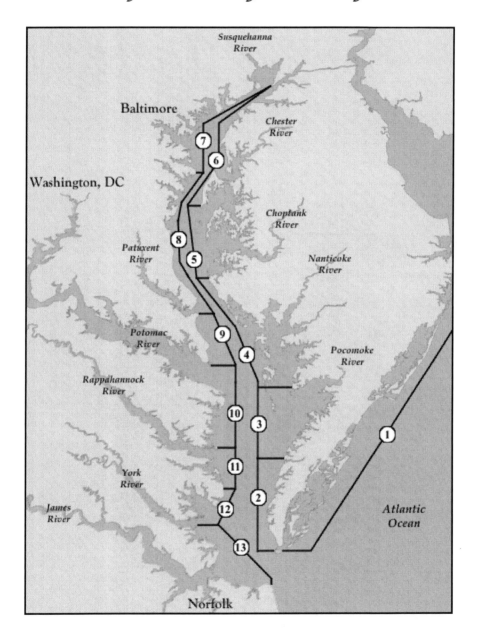

The 13 Oyster Growing Zones of the Chesapeake Bay

Oyster Growing Zone	Salinity Range	Saltiness	Buttery/Creamy	Sweetness
1-Seaside Zone	28-32 ppt	9	3	3
	Initial bold saltiness mellowing into a taste of sweet butter/cream at the finish			
2-Cape Charles Zone	18-22 ppt	7	3	3
	Salty and creamy with mellow sweetness and a quick finish			
3-Pocomoke River Zone	16-18 ppt	5	1	3
	Classic oyster flavor with balanced salt and sweet with a savory finish			
4-Nanticoke River Zone	15-18 ppt	5	3	3
	Clean, buttery ocean flavor and a sweet complex finish			
5-Choptank River Zone	12-15 ppt	4	3	3
	Sweet buttery flavor with moderate salinity and a clean crisp finish			
6-Chester River Zone	1-13 ppt	2	4	2
	Sweet melon-cucumber taste with a crisp, slightly briny finish			
7-Susquehanna River Zone	1-10 ppt			
	No oysters farmed in this zone			
8-Patuxent River Zone	10-17 ppt	4	3	3
	Mild, slightly sweet lending to a mellow finish			
9-Southern Maryland Zone	15-18 ppt	5	3	3
	Crisp, slightly salty with smooth hints of cucumber finish			
10-Potomac River Zone	10-17 ppt	5	2	2
	Sweetwater oyster with a light cream taste			
11-Rappahannock River Zone	16-18 ppt	5	3	3
	Lightly salty with easily distinguished cream or butter and a pleasant slight minerality			
12-York River Zone	16-18 ppt	5	2	2
	Mild saltiness moving to a sweet finish			
13-James River Zone	16-30 ppt	8	2	3
	Salty with sweetness and a smooth finish			

1-2 Barely Perceptible • 3-4 Slightly • 5-6 Moderate • 7-8 Very Noticeable • 9 Strong

Chesapeake Oyster Taste Chart

Oyster Tasting Wheel

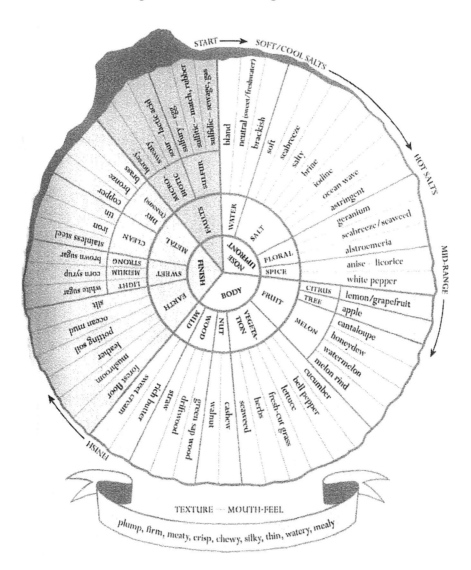

Source: Consider the Oyster, A Shucker's Field Guide, Patrick McMurray

Chesapeake Oyster Taste Chart

Oysters are presented in brand name order with taste descriptions provided by aquafarms. Those in italics are not from aquafarms and growing zone descriptions are provided instead.

Chesapeake Oyster Brand	Salinity Range	Oyster Growing Zone	Taste Description
Avery's Pearls	18-22 ppt	2-Cape Charles Zone	Petite oyster with incredible pure brine finish
Barcat Oysters	16-18 ppt	11-Rappahannock River Zone	*Lightly salty with easily distinguished cream or butter and a pleasant slight minerality*
Barren Island Oysters	15-18 ppt	4-Nanticoke River Zone	Super clean and buttery flavor with just the right amount of salt and complexity to not overpower its sweet finish
Battle Creek Oysters	28-32 ppt	1-Seaside Zone	High salinity, bold saltiness, mild-sweet finish
Bay Breeze Oysters	16-18 ppt	12-York River Zone	Salty oysters with slight sweetness and a smooth finish
Bevans Oysters	10-17 ppt	10-Potomac River Zone	*Sweetwater oyster with a light cream taste*
Big Island Oysters	16-18 ppt	12-York River Zone	Perfect blend of salty, sweet and buttery
Black Horse Oysters	15-18 ppt	4-Nanticoke River Zone	Delicate balance of the salt of the ocean with a hint of sweetness
Black Pearl Oysters	28-32 ppt	1-Seaside Zone	*Initial bold saltiness mellowing into a taste of sweet butter/cream at the finish*
Black Walnut Point Oysters	12-15 ppt	5-Choptank River Zone	*Sweet buttery flavor with moderate salinity and a clean crisp finish*
Broadwater Oysters	18-22 ppt	2-Cape Charles Zone	Mouthwatering briny with hints of cedar and spice and everything nice
Calvert Crest Oysters	10-17 ppt	8-Patuxent River Zone	*Mild, slightly sweet lending to a mellow finish*

Chesapeake Oyster Taste Chart

Chesapeake Oyster Brand	Salinity Range	Oyster Growing Zone	Taste Description
Cannon Cove Oysters	16-18 ppt	12-York River Zone	Medium salinity, smooth body, clean finish
Cape Charles Carpe Diem Premium Oysters	28-32 ppt	1-Seaside Zone	*Initial bold saltiness mellowing into a taste of sweet butter/cream at the finish*
Chapel Creek Oysters	16-18 ppt	1-Seaside Zone	Buttery mineral rich taste with a crisp light finish and the right amount of salt
Chesapeake Gold Oysters	15-18 ppt	11-Rappahannock River Zone	Plump, full-bodied with a clean, strong ocean flavor and a sweet complex finish
Chincoteague Atlantics Choice Oysters	28-32 ppt	4-Nanticoke River Zone	*Initial bold saltiness mellowing into a taste of sweet butter/cream at the finish*
Chincoteague Cultured Salt Oysters	28-32 ppt	1-Seaside Zone	Salt, salt, and more salt!
Choice of Chesapeake Bay Oysters	16-18 ppt	1-Seaside Zone	*Lightly salty with easily distinguished cream or butter and a pleasant slight minerality*
Choptank Sweets	12-15 ppt	11-Rappahannock River Zone	Full-bodied, meaty, medium salinity, very clean
Chunu Cultured Oysters	28-32 ppt	5-Choptank River Zone	High salinity up front quickly transitioning to a sweet grassy finish
Church Point Oysters	16-30 ppt	1-Seaside Zone	*Salty oyster with sweetness and a smooth finish*
Dandylicious Oysters	16-18 ppt	13-James River Zone	*Mild saltiness moving to a sweet finish*
Double Dee Oysters	10-17 ppt	12-York River Zone	Medium salinity, full cup with beautiful presentation, delicate minerality and creamy finish
Double T Oysters	10-17 ppt	10-Potomac River Zone	*Sweetwater oyster with a light cream taste*

Chesapeake Oyster Taste Chart

Chesapeake Oyster Brand	Salinity Range	Oyster Growing Zone	Taste Description
Eagle Flats	16-18 ppt	10-Potomac River Zone	Buttery balance between savory and sweet, containing just the right amount of salinity to produce a crisp finish
Fat 'N Happy Oysters	10-17 ppt	12-York River Zone	*Sweetwater oyster with a light cream taste*
Fat Beech Oysters	15-18 ppt	10-Potomac River Zone	Buttery and complex
Fleet's Bay Oysters	16-18 ppt	4-Nanticoke River Zone	Slight salinity, very plump body with a creamy buttery finish
Fleets Island Oysters	16-18 ppt	11-Rappahannock River Zone	*Lightly salty with easily distinguished cream or butter and a pleasant slight minerality*
Gloucester Point Oysters	16-18 ppt	11-Rappahannock River Zone	A taste of the ocean, with a buttery finish
Grand Pearl Oysters	16-18 ppt	12-York River Zone	Mild, briny salt-flavored taste which melts into a buttery and sweet, distinctive finish
Happy Oysters	10-17 ppt	3-Pocomoke River Zone	Sweet buttery/creamy, medium salinity, clean, fresh
Hayden's Reef Oysters	10-17 ppt	10-Potomac River Zone	Mild, sweet flavor and light brine
Hollywood Oysters	10-17 ppt	10-Potomac River Zone	Medium salinity with a hint of mineral and a creamy cucumber taste
Holy Grail Oysters	15-18 ppt	8-Patuxent River Zone	Heavy ocean flavor, sweet complex finish
HongaTonk Oysters	15-18 ppt	4-Nanticoke River Zone	Medium salinity; everyone who tries them likes them
Huckleberry Oysters	15-18 ppt	4-Nanticoke River Zone	Soft-salt, refreshing taste with a fresh, clean finish
Indian Rock Oysters	28-32 ppt	9-Southern Maryland Zone	Nicely briny with a clean finish
Island Girl Oysters	10-17 ppt	1-Seaside Zone	Medium salinity with a hint of sweetness
Kellum Oysters	16-18 ppt	8-Patuxent River Zone	Plump, delicate, tender, slightly salty

Chesapeake Oyster Lovers Handbook

Chesapeake Oyster Taste Chart

Chesapeake Oyster Brand	Salinity Range	Oyster Growing Zone	Taste Description
Lineback Oysters	15-18 ppt	11-Rappahannock River Zone	*Crisp, slightly salty with smooth hints of cucumber finish*
Little Bitches	18-22 ppt	9-Southern Maryland Zone	Petite cocktail oyster, full flavored, a lot of punch in a small package
Little Wicomico Oysters	10-17 ppt	2-Cape Charles Zone	*Sweetwater oyster with a light cream taste*
Lone Point Oysters	16-18 ppt	10-Potomac River Zone	*Mild saltiness moving to a sweet finish*
Lynnhaven Oysters	16-30 ppt	12-York River Zone	Fresh, salty, one of a kind
Lynnhaven River Oysters	16-30 ppt	13-James River Zone	*Salty oyster with sweetness and a smooth finish*
M&S Charmer Oysters	15-18 ppt	13-James River Zone	Soft-salt, refreshing taste with a fresh, clean finish
Madhouse Oysters	15-18 ppt	9-Southern Maryland Zone	Delicate balance of the salt of the ocean with a hint of sweetness
Main Stream Oysters	28-32 ppt	4-Nanticoke River Zone	*Initial bold saltiness mellowing into a taste of sweet butter/cream at the finish*
McKinney's Island Oysters	16-18 ppt	1-Seaside Zone	*Classic oyster flavor with balanced salt and sweet with a savory finish*
Misty Point Oysters	28-32 ppt	3-Pocomoke River Zone	High salinity up front that fades into bright, sweet hits of celery and grass
Mobjack Bay Oysters	16-18 ppt	1-Seaside Zone	*Mild saltiness moving to a sweet finish*
Mojo Oysters	28-32 ppt	12-York River Zone	Salty, briny, crisp, Maryland's saltiest oyster
Nandua Oysters	16-18 ppt	1-Seaside Zone	*Classic oyster flavor with balanced salt and sweet with a savory finish*
Nassawadox Salts	18-22 ppt	3-Pocomoke River Zone	Balanced salt, estuarine flavors with strong hints of the Atlantic
NautiGirl Oysters	16-18 ppt	2-Cape Charles Zone	Sweet buttery taste with a medium saltiness and a rich, clean finish

Chesapeake Oyster Taste Chart

Chesapeake Oyster Brand	Salinity Range	Oyster Growing Zone	Taste Description
New Point Oysters	16-18 ppt	11-Rappahannock River Zone	Mild saltiness moving to a sweet finish
Old Black Salts	28-32 ppt	12-York River Zone	Bold sea-side brininess with a smooth, clean follow-through
Olde Salts	28-32 ppt	1-Seaside Zone	Bold sea-side brininess with a smooth, clean follow-through
Orchard Point Oysters	1-13 ppt	1-Seaside Zone	Sweet melon-cucumber flavor with a crisp, slightly briny finish
Parrot Island Oysters	16-18 ppt	6-Chester River Zone	Mildly salty, slightly sweet
Patty's Fatty's	10-17 ppt	11-Rappahannock River Zone	Mild, slightly sweet lending to a mellow finish
Pepper Creek Oysters	16-18 ppt	8-Patuxent River Zone	Mild saltiness moving to a sweet finish
Pleasure House Oysters	16-30 ppt	12-York River Zone	Good up front salt taste followed by a sweet body with cucumber, grassy and seaweed highlights
Point Lookout Oysters	15-18 ppt	13-James River Zone	Crisp, slightly salty with smooth hints of cucumber finish
Poquoson Oysters	16-18 ppt	9-Southern Maryland Zone	Mild saltiness moving to a sweet finish
Rappahannock River Oysters	16-18 ppt	12-York River Zone	Sweet, buttery, full-bodied taste with a refreshingly clean, crisp finish
Revel's Island Bay Oysters	28-32 ppt	11-Rappahannock River Zone	Initial bold saltiness mellowing into a taste of sweet butter/cream at the finish
Ropewalk Liberty Oysters	16-18 ppt	1-Seaside Zone	Classic oyster flavor with balanced salt and sweet with a savory finish
Ruby Salts Oysters	18-22 ppt	3-Pocomoke River Zone	Fresh, plump, salty, juicy, good!
Salt Works Oysters	18-22 ppt	2-Cape Charles Zone	Salty and creamy with mellow sweetness and a quick finish

Chesapeake Oyster Taste Chart

Chesapeake Oyster Brand	Salinity Range	Oyster Growing Zone	Taste Description
Sandy Point Oysters	18-22 ppt	2-Cape Charles Zone	Salty and creamy with mellow sweetness and a quick finish
Saxis Island Bullets	16-18 ppt	2-Cape Charles Zone	Classic oyster flavor with balanced salt and sweet with a savory finish
Seaford Oysters	16-18 ppt	3-Pocomoke River Zone	Delicious salty southern Bay taste
Sea-Licious Oysters	16-18 ppt	12-York River Zone	Mild saltiness moving to a sweet finish
Sewansecott Oysters	28-32 ppt	12-York River Zone	Initial briny burst of flavor mellowing to a sweet, delicate finish
Ship Point Oysters	16-18 ppt	1-Seaside Zone	Mild saltiness moving to a sweet finish
Shooting Point Salts	28-32 ppt	12-York River Zone	Incredible brine untarnished by freshets, buttery sweet finish
Shore Thing Oysters	10-17 ppt	1-Seaside Zone	Deep cup, mild to medium salt, clean taste
Skinny Dipper Oysters	15-18 ppt	10-Potomac River Zone	Soft-salt, refreshing taste with a fresh, clean finish
Skipjack Oysters	10-17 ppt	9-Southern Maryland Zone	Medium salinity, delicate minerality with creamy finish
Snow Hill Oysters	28-32 ppt	10-Potomac River Zone	Cool ocean salt cut ever so slightly with a fresh-water sweetness
Stingray Oysters	16-18 ppt	1-Seaside Zone	Sweet and mildly briny with a clean, crisp finish
Stump Cove Oysters	12-15 ppt	11-Rappahannock River Zone	Sweet buttery flavor with moderate salinity and a clean crisp finish
Sweet Jesus Oysters	10-17 ppt	5-Choptank River Zone	Medium salinity with a hint of mineral and a creamy cucumber taste
Sweet Petites	10-17 ppt	8-Patuxent River Zone	Mild salinity, delicate cup with petite presentation and a fresh finish
38° North Oysters	15-18 ppt	10-Potomac River Zone	Firm and meaty with just the right balance of salinity

Chesapeake Oyster Taste Chart

Chesapeake Oyster Brand	Salinity Range	Oyster Growing Zone	Taste Description
Toby Island Oysters	28-32 ppt	9-Southern Maryland Zone	Salty with a sweet finish
Tom's Cove Oysters	28-32 ppt	1-Seaside Zone	*Initial bold saltiness mellowing into a taste of sweet butter/cream at the finish*
Ugly Oysters	15-18 ppt	1-Seaside Zone	Clean and buttery, but a little rough around the edges; they've got great personalities
Uncle Ernie's Oysters	15-18 ppt	4-Nanticoke River Zone	*Clean, buttery ocean flavor and a sweet complex finish*
Urbanna Creek Oysters	16-18 ppt	4-Nanticoke River Zone	*Lightly salty with easily distinguished cream or butter and a pleasant slight minerality*
War Shore Oysters	16-18 ppt	11-Rappahannock River Zone	Light to medium salinity, crisp body, savory sweet finish
Watch House Point Oysters	18-22 ppt	3-Pocomoke River Zone	Salty upfront followed by hints of cucumber and melon
White Stone Oysters	16-18 ppt	2-Cape Charles Zone	*Lightly salty with easily distinguished cream or butter and a pleasant slight minerality*
Whitewood Cove Oysters	15-18 ppt	11-Rappahannock River Zone	*Clean, buttery ocean flavor and a sweet complex finish*
Windmill Point Oysters	16-18 ppt	4-Nanticoke River Zone	*Lightly salty with easily distinguished cream or butter and a pleasant slight minerality*
Winter Harbor Oysters	16-18 ppt	11-Rappahannock River Zone	Deep cup, iron filing flecked shell, with a mild briny taste
Witch Duck Oysters	16-30 ppt	12-York River Zone	Simple salty taste of the Bay
York River Oysters	16-18 ppt	13-James River Zone	Medium salinity, plump body, savory sweet finish
Yorkster Oysters	16-18 ppt	12-York River Zone	*Mild saltiness moving to a sweet finish*

Who is Citizen Pride?

There's a special pride each of us take in our hometown and iconic symbols that are unique to where we live. We call it "Citizen Pride" and our artwork in print, on canvas, flags and note cards offer an original and meaningful way to share and display it.

Joe and Eva Barsin at the Maryland Bay Plate's unveiling ceremony.

Illustrations by Joe Barsin are well known since he created the **Maryland Bay license plate** and the recent series of posters promoting the *Annapolis Film Festival*, along with numerous magazine and commissioned artwork.

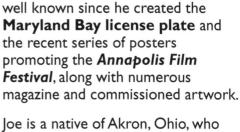

Annapolis Film Festival Poster

Joe is a native of Akron, Ohio, who graduated from Kent State University with a degree in graphic design. He and his wife, Eva, started their own design firm, JEB Design, Inc., in 1998, and continue to work from home while raising their two boys.

Take a look at Joe's work at *CitizenPride.com* to see what stirs your sense of citizen pride. We have a full line of gifts and products featuring Joe Barsin's work.

CitizenPride.com
facebook.com/CitizenPrideUSA

Show your Pride!

Citizen Pride art products offer you a unique way to express your pride and the places you visit.

Our Products Include:
**Garden & House Flags
Door Mats • Canvas Wall Art
Print • Notecards • Postcards
Magnets • Stickers**

Visit **CitizenPride.com** to see our full line of gifts and products. Featured here are some of the illustrations offered.

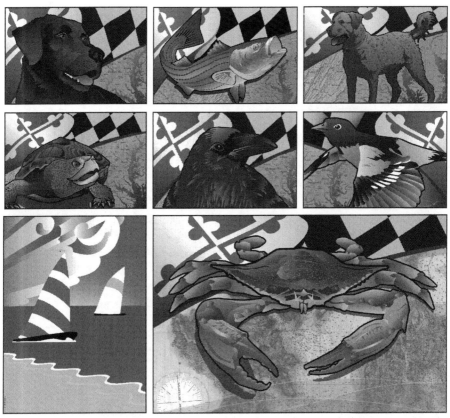

Illustration by local artist, Joe Barsin.
Barsin created the Maryland Bay license plate.

CitizenPride.com
facebook.com/CitizenPrideUSA

CITIZEN PRIDE®

Made in the USA
Middletown, DE
09 October 2016